BALLOTS AND BANDWAGONS

CHOOSING THE
CANDIDATES

BALLOTS AND BANDWAGONS

CHOOSING THE CANDIDATES
by George Sullivan

CAMPAIGNS AND ELECTIONS
by George Sullivan

THE PRESIDENCY
by Richard M. Pious

BALLOTS AND BANDWAGONS

CHOOSING THE CANDIDATES

GEORGE SULLIVAN

Silver Burdett Press

Design by R^studio T.
Manufactured in the United States of America.

Lib. ed. 10 9 8 7 6 5 4 3 2 1

Paper ed. 10 9 8 7 6 5 4 3 2 1

Library of Congress Cataloging-in-Publication Data

Sullivan, George.
    Choosing the candidates / George Sullivan
    p.   cm. — (Ballots and bandwagons)
    Includes index.
    Summary: Examines the history and current practice of political parties' nomina-
tion of presidential candidates, emphasizing campaign strategy and tactics, and the
working of the primary system and party conventions.
    1. Presidents — United States — Nomination — Juvenile literature. [1. Presidents
—Nomination. 2. Politics, Practical.] I. Title. II. Series: Sullivan, George. Ballots
and bandwagons.
JK521.S85   1991b
324.5'6' 0973 — dc20   91-14417
                                                                           CIP
                                                                           AC

        ISBN 0-382-24314-5 (LSB)   ISBN 0-382-24319-6 (paper)

CONTENTS

On the campaign trail in 1988, George and Barbara Bush wave to well-wishers during the Fourth of July parade in Wyandotte, Michigan.

CHAPTER ONE

THE WAY THINGS WORK

Every four years on the Tuesday after the first Monday in November, one hundred million or so Americans exercise what is their greatest political power — choosing a President.

Article II, Section 1 of the Constitution, which deals with the qualifications for the presidency, says that Presidents must be natural-born citizens, at least thirty-five years old, and have lived in the United States for at least fourteen years. By those standards, tens of millions of Americans are qualified to occupy the office. But the voting machines and ballots on which the voters register their choices contain the names of only two persons with a realistic chance of winning.

The sorting-out process in which the millions who are eligible are reduced to a handful is one of the critical functions of the nation's political parties. A candidate must compete against other members of his or her party to get nominated. It is a long and complicated process. At times, it confuses even those who are most closely involved in it.

Some people say that the 1992 campaign for the Democratic presidential nomination began on a November Saturday in 1988. That is when Jesse Jackson went to Des Moines, Iowa, to speak to a farmers' group. In other words, Jackson fired the opening gun of his campaign almost four full years before the nominating convention was to take place.

In his speech in Des Moines, Jackson was looking ahead to the 1992 Iowa caucuses. A caucus is a meeting of small groups of party members in which they indicate their presidential choice. The Iowa caucuses are the first official event in the process of winning the Democratic presidential nomination, and they have taken on enormous importance in recent years. Do well in Iowa, most candidates believe, and the world will beat a path to your door. By starting early, Jackson was hoping to gain an edge on his rivals, although at the time he wasn't quite sure who those rivals were going to be.

Americans select a President every four years (in years that can be divided by four, such as 1996, 1980, 1964, and 1888). In the past, there were long breaks between one presidential campaign and the one that followed. Those days have gone the way of home-delivered milk. In the past twenty or so years, the gap between the campaigns has closed. Nowadays, at about the same time the newly elected President is taking the oath of office, the campaign to choose a successor is likely to be getting underway.

Primaries and Caucuses

The reason that winning the nomination is now a four-year struggle has to do with the changes that have taken place in the nominating process. At one time, presidential candidates were chosen at the national conventions held by the Democrats and Republicans.

Nowadays, it's different. Primary elections are held in most states. In a primary, voters choose delegates to the national conventions. At the conventions, the delegates cast their ballots for the voters' choices.

In 1988, more delegates to national conventions were picked by means of primary elections than ever before. Democrats had primaries in thirty-three states; Republicans in thirty-seven.

Instead of having primaries, some states, such as Iowa, hold meetings of small groups of party members where they vote for candidates. Each party member gets one vote. As mentioned previously, these meetings are the caucuses. Alaska, Maine, and Michigan were other states that selected delegates by the caucus method in 1988.

The primaries and caucuses are held during the first six months of the presidential election year, with each state choosing its own election date. New Hampshire traditionally holds the first primary. In 1988, the primary-caucus calendar was as follows:

* Late January—the Michigan State Republican Convention, the first contest to select delegates to the national convention
* Early February—the Iowa caucuses
* Mid-February—the New Hampshire primary
* Second Tuesday in March—Super Tuesday; sixteen primaries in mostly southern and border states
* Late March—primary voting in Illinois, a key industrial state
* Early to mid-April—crucial primaries in Indiana, Pennsylvania, and Ohio
* May—several western state primaries yielding 107 votes for both the Democrats and Republicans
* Early June—four more primaries, including big delegate contests in New Jersey and California, ending the primary season
* July and August—Democratic and Republican National Conventions
* September—Labor Day, the traditional opening day of the general election campaign
* Mid-September to mid-October—televised debates between candidates
* Second Tuesday in November—election day

Each party's national convention now merely endorses the results of the primary and caucus voting. Even though a roll-call vote of the states is taken, everyone knows what the outcome is going to be. The last time there was any suspense to the voting at a national convention was in 1976, when Ronald Reagan, in his first bid for the Republican nomination, squared off against President Gerald Ford, a matchup Ford won.

These changes in the nominating process have had important implications. Prospective candidates can now connect directly with the voters through television, sidestepping political leaders. The bosses who once ruled national conventions are no longer in control when it comes to choosing candidates.

The emphasis on primaries and caucuses has also made for more active and much earlier campaigning. The fact that Jesse Jackson, in quest of the 1992 Democratic nomination, journeyed to Des Moines in 1988 to speak to a group of Iowa farmers is evidence of that.

Most political observers and, indeed, most voters agree that the process of selecting candidates to run for President lasts too long and costs too much. But no one has put forth any practical solutions to these problems.

It's different in other countries. In Great Britain, for instance, once an election is called, the campaigning usually lasts about three weeks. Free television air time is allowed, with the amount based on the strength shown by each party in the previous election. The stronger the showing, the more television time a party receives. In a national election, parties are not limited as to how much money they can spend.

In Germany, campaigns are permitted to start ten months before election day. Political parties are allowed paid time on government television, with the amount based on the number of seats the party has in the government. No limits are imposed on campaign spending.

In Israel, campaigns generally last from three to four months. There is no limit on campaign spending. Each party is allowed government money in proportion to its seats in parliament. Television advertising is also allotted according to each party's strength.

In other countries of Western Europe, limits are placed on paid political advertising. At the same time, television and radio stations are required to make time available to political parties.

That concept might not work in this country. Mandating what programming television and radio must carry would probably become a freedom-of-the-press issue. Serious legal problems could result.

Short or Long Campaigns?

Some critics say that if the election campaign were shortened, enormous benefits would result. Candidates would be able to cut campaign expenditures. Money would thus play less of a role for those seeking office.

The boredom factor would be reduced, too. There might be greater interest in a campaign that lasted only a few months as opposed to one that seemingly goes on without end. Increased voter turnout could be the result.

On the other hand, long campaigns do serve a purpose. They help to educate voters. When Ronald Reagan opposed Jimmy Carter in 1980 and Walter Mondale in 1984, it made people think about the direction the government was taking. Reagan favored "getting the government off of the people's backs." His opponents felt there was no need to. Taxes and military spending were other important issues discussed in those campaigns.

When Richard Nixon ran against Hubert Humphrey in 1968 and George McGovern in 1972, it made voters think deeply about the Vietnam War. The presidential campaigns of George Wallace and Robert Kennedy, also in 1968, helped to make voters more sensitive to racial issues.

As the process of selecting candidates becomes longer and more drawn out, it places greater and greater stress on the individuals. In 1960, John F. Kennedy ran in only seven primaries. Today, a candidate campaigns in about five times that number. The constant demands of television and the press must be satisfied. Pressure groups, which keep growing in number and variety, also impose strains.

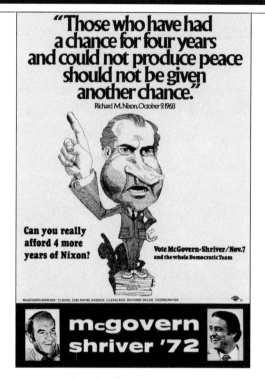

"Those who have had a chance for four years and could not produce peace should not be given another chance."

Richard M. Nixon, October 9, 1968

Can you really afford 4 more years of Nixon?

Vote McGovern-Shriver/Nov.7 and the whole Democratic Team

McGOVERN/SHRIVER '72 OHIO, 2340 PAYNE AVENUE, CLEVELAND, RICHARD SKLAR, COORDINATOR

mcgovern shriver '72

The war in Vietnam was the chief issue when Richard Nixon faced George McGovern in the 1972 election campaign.

Senator Walter Mondale of Minnesota sought the 1976 Democratic presidential nomination but withdrew from the race in 1974 because he couldn't take the pressure. "Look at the schedules, travel times, the absence of weekends for rest," Mondale told the *New Yorker.* "It's not just the physical fatigue, it's the emotional pressure of it all.

"I didn't want to do it. I had to think about whether you should also have some time to be with friends, families, to fish, to have a little balance in your life. . . ."

Mondale later changed his mind. During the early 1980s, he campaigned again for the nomination, which he won in 1984, only to be defeated in the general election by Ronald Reagan.

Speaker of the House Thomas S. Foley, who represented eastern Washington in the House of Representatives for more than twenty-five years beginning in 1964, was once described by the *New York*

Times as "the kind of man whom people are always trying to persuade to run for President." The fifty-nine-year-old Foley was known as a fair-minded individual, dignified but not stuffy. He was also skilled as a television performer. In 1986, Robert S. Strauss, the one-time chairman of the Democratic National Committee, said of him, "There's no one in America more qualified for the presidency than Tom Foley."

But Foley had no ambition to become President. He wanted no part of national politics, in fact. "My future, such as it is, lies in the House," said Foley. "To run for the office of President, you have to have an enormous passion. You have to want it with a compelling urgency. You have to be prepared to sacrifice all kinds of things—financial security, your privacy, family well-being—on the altar of that desire, and even then the odds will be profoundly against you.

"I know of any number of people who I think would make good Presidents," Foley added, "even great Presidents, who are deterred from running by the torture candidates are obliged to put themselves through."

Every four years, after a President is elected, countless suggestions are offered as to how the system might be changed. No one disputes the fact that the existing process is "torture" for the candidates. At times, it seems to be the worst possible way of doing things. But it appears to be better than any other system that has been tried.

CHAPTER TWO

HOW WE GOT THIS WAY

I n the early days of the nation, presidential candidates were not nominated the way Democrats and Republicans nominate candidates today, that is, by means of caucuses, primary elections, and national conventions. The Constitution says nothing about how candidates are to be chosen. The system in use today developed more or less by trial and error.

The method to be used in choosing the President was a big problem at the Constitutional Convention of 1787. The Convention rejected the idea that Congress elect the nation's chief executive. The feeling was that the President then would be under the control of the legislative branch of government.

Most of the framers of the Constitution believed that presidential nominations should be the responsibility of the individuals who ran the national government, not the citizens at large. So the proposal that the people directly elect the President was also rejected.

The Convention finally agreed to choose the President by means of a body of presiden-

*George Washington was chosen as the nation's first President
by the balloting of electors.*

tial electors. The number of electors for each state would be equal
to the number of senators and representatives to which the state was
entitled.

On February 4, 1789, the electoral college, as the body of electors came to be called, met for the first time in New York City. Ten
states sent sixty-nine electors. Different methods had been used for
choosing them. In five states—Connecticut, Delaware, Georgia,
New Jersey, and South Carolina—the electors were chosen by state
legislatures. Three states—Maryland, Pennsylvania, and Virginia
—held popular elections. Massachusetts had a system that com-
bined a popular election and appointment by the state legislature.
In New Hampshire, the electors were named by the state senate.

Each elector cast one of his two votes for George Washington,
who received 69 of the 138 votes and became President. The other
69 votes were divided among eleven other candidates. John Adams
of Massachusetts received more of the remaining votes than anyone
else and as the runner-up became Vice-President.

Before Washington's first term ended, it was necessary to elect a President and Vice-President for a second administration. Electors met again and produced much the same results—Washington and Adams were reelected, Washington receiving 132 of the 264 votes cast; Adams got 77 votes, with the balance of the votes going to other candidates.

After Washington had served his second term, he declined to serve a third time. Some procedure then had to be decided upon for nominating candidates for the next election.

Political Parties Emerge

Times were changing by 1796. Political parties were becoming more important. Although parties had not been listed on the ballots in the first election and their very idea was opposed by Washington, both he and Adams were known as Federalists. They favored a strong national government.

The Federalists were men of wealth and position—landowners, merchants, and bankers. They supported the new Constitution. Those who opposed them, the Anti-Federalists, mostly farmers and local politicians, feared the Constitution and the strong central government for which it provided.

James Madison, an Anti-Federalist while serving in Congress in the late 1700s, wanted a government that gave greater power to the people. But Alexander Hamilton, the leader of the Federalists, opposed the idea. Hamilton told Madison, "Your people is a great beast."

Before the election of 1796, those who called themselves Federalists and who had been in power for almost eight years during Washington's two terms of office, met to discuss their policies and plans and to agree on presidential and vice-presidential candidates. In this meeting, the original caucus, they decided to throw their support to Vice-President John Adams. To attract electoral votes from the South, they added Thomas Pinckney, a South Carolina diplomat.

The Anti-Federalist group in Congress decided to support

Thomas Jefferson and Aaron Burr. This group became known as Democratic-Republicans.

The Constitution did not make any provision for these congressional caucuses. The results they produced represented the views only of those who held political power at the time. There was no consideration of the will of the people.

And there still was no single method for choosing electors. Each state had its own system. Some electors were chosen by state legislators, some by popular vote, and some by other methods.

The election of 1796 produced bizarre results. Electors from sixteen states cast 276 votes. The four candidates receiving the greatest number of electoral votes were:

CANDIDATE	*PARTY*	*NUMBER OF VOTES*
John Adams	Federalist	71
Thomas Jefferson	Democratic-Republican	68
Thomas Pinckney	Federalist	59
Aaron Burr	Democratic-Republican	30

So it was that the new President, John Adams, represented one party, while his Vice-President, Thomas Jefferson, represented the rival party. If the President were to die in office, his successor would be a person holding completely different views. The framers of the Constitution had never imagined anything like this happening. Obviously, the Constitution was going to have to be changed.

In 1800, the system again produced controversial results. John Adams hoped to be reelected. But opposition to Federalist policies was stiffening. The Democratic-Republicans rallied behind Thomas Jefferson of Virginia and Aaron Burr of New York. The Federalist congressmen, meeting in the Senate chamber, decided to support Adams for a second term and, as his running mate, Charles Cotesworth Pinckney of South Carolina.

The electors cast 276 votes—with these results:

CANDIDATE	PARTY	NUMBER OF VOTES
Thomas Jefferson	Democratic-Republican	73
Aaron Burr	Democratic-Republican	73
John Adams	Federalist	65
Charles Cotesworth Pinckney	Federalist	64
John Jay	Federalist	1

Because Jefferson and Burr each received the same number of votes, the election was referred to the House of Representatives to decide which candidate would be President and which Vice-President. The outcome would not be as ticklish as 1796, for the two candidates were both Democratic-Republicans. It was a contest of personalities, not political factions.

The balloting began on February 11, 1801. The representatives did not vote individually but by state groups, with each state having one vote. It took about a week and thirty-six ballots to arrive at a choice. Ten states voted for Jefferson, four for Burr, and two voted blank. Thomas Jefferson was declared to be President and Aaron Burr Vice-President.

Changing Election Procedures

To avoid such tangled situations in the future, election procedures were changed. The change was mandated by the Twelfth Amendment to the Constitution, which went into effect on November 6, 1804. It provided that the President and Vice-President be voted for separately. The amendment almost guarantees that the President and Vice-President will always be of the same party.

During the 1820s, the nation went through a period of important change. From George Washington to John Quincy Adams, American Presidents had been gentlemen of education and privilege. Washington had died in 1799, John Adams and Thomas Jefferson in 1826.

The 1820s were the time of the farmer, the worker, the frontiersman, the so-called common man. The period was typified by Andrew Jackson, an orphan boy born in South Carolina. By the time he was twenty, Jackson was a backwoods lawyer. At the age of thirty, he represented the newly formed state of Tennessee in the United States Senate.

Jackson went on to become a military hero in the War of 1812. After a stirring victory over the British at the Battle of New Orleans, people began mentioning Jackson as a future President. He later won even greater fame as an Indian fighter in Florida.

Jackson was one of four choices in 1824, all of whom were Democratic-Republicans. The Federalists had faded from the scene. Each of the four represented one region or another of the United States. Besides Jackson, with his Tennessee roots, the candidates included Henry Clay, from Kentucky, which, like Tennessee, was then regarded as a "western" state; John Quincy Adams, from the Northeast; and William H. Crawford, from the Southeast.

Jackson was nominated by the Tennessee legislature and a number of conventions in various parts of the country. Clay was nominated by the Kentucky legislature and several other state legislatures, and Adams by the legislatures of most of the New England states.

Crawford's case was different. A former senator from Georgia, and later secretary of war and then secretary of the treasury, Crawford was nominated by a caucus held in the chamber of the House of Representatives. But the conference was poorly attended, and immediately afterward, Crawford's opponents attacked his nomination as undemocratic and unconstitutional. "King Caucus" became a hot campaign issue, and arguments for and against the caucuses filled newspapers of the day.

In part, at least, the distaste for the caucus system had grown as the nation expanded westward and new territories were added. New political leaders, popular in frontier areas, complained that they were hardly known by the senators and representatives in Washington, those who were responsible for caucus choices.

The caucus was the chief issue of the election of 1824. To many people, the congressional caucus had come to imply a decision made by a handful of Washington politicians, without any regard for the opinions or feelings of large segments of the population. Crawford's election bid was damaged because he was so closely identified with "King Caucus."

By the fall of 1824, when the twenty-four states began choosing presidential electors, it was apparent that Jackson and Adams were the leading candidates. These were the final results:

CANDIDATE	POPULAR VOTES	ELECTORAL VOTES
Andrew Jackson	152,933	99
John Quincy Adams	115,696	84
William H. Crawford	46,979	41
Henry Clay	47,136	37

Although Jackson led in the voting, he failed to win a majority of the electoral votes. Again, an election was put into the hands of the House of Representatives. There the supporters of Henry Clay switched their votes to Adams, and Adams was elected.

At first, Jackson accepted the loss gracefully. Then Adams announced that he was appointing Clay to be his secretary of state. Jackson became enraged. He believed that he had been the victim of a "deal," that Clay had made a "corrupt bargain" in delivering his support to Adams in return for the cabinet post.

Jackson resigned from the Senate and headed back to Tennessee to begin preparing for the next election. "The people have been cheated," he fumed.

Between 1824 and 1828, the number of Americans eligible to vote grew by leaps and bounds. Many states decided that presidential electors should be chosen by popular vote, instead of being selected by state legislatures. By 1828, only two states—South Carolina and Delaware—had failed to provide for the selection of electors by popular vote. In addition, many states removed property ownership as a qualification for voting. As a result of these changes,

The election of 1828, won by Andrew Jackson, was the first in which great masses of people voted.

the election of 1828 was the first in which great masses of people voted. (Still, it was only adult white males who were eligible to vote in the 1820s. Women were not granted the right to vote until 1920. American blacks, to a great extent, were denied the right to vote until the passage of voting rights legislation during the 1960s and 1970s. Those eighteen years and older got the right to vote with the passage of the Twenty-sixth Amendment to the Constitution in 1971.)

There were no caucus nominations in 1828. Jackson and his supporters argued that the popular vote showed that congressional caucuses did not represent the wishes of the people. "King Caucus" was dead.

For the election of 1828, all the nominations were made by state legislatures. Jackson was nominated by the Tennessee legislature in October 1825, but even before that he had been receiving endorsements from conventions and mass meetings in other parts of the country.

Jackson and his followers believed political parties were vital to the workings of a political democracy. They established party organizations in all twenty-four states, and improved and expanded the committee system that managed the details of Jackson's campaign — raising money; arranging dinners and parades; and providing pamphlets, leaflets, and other printed materials.

Adams and his supporters had none of Jackson's enthusiasm for political parties. Adams himself, who had been nominated for reelection by state legislatures and special conventions in New England, believed that parties and their quarrels were a threat to the stability of the nation. In comparison with Jackson's Democratic-Republican party, later, simply, the Democratic party, the National Republican party of Adams and Clay sadly lacked in organization and leadership.

Admission tickets for the 1980 Democratic convention in New York City with portraits of Jefferson (left) and Jackson (right) indicate the party's roots.

The turnout in 1828 was three times as great as in 1824. Jackson won 647,231 popular votes and 178 electoral votes to Adams's 509,097 popular votes and 83 electoral votes.

The First Political Convention

By now it was obvious that some other method would have to be decided upon to sort out each party's presidential contenders. The method that evolved was the national party convention, meeting every four years.

The very first political convention to nominate a candidate was held in September 1831, when the Anti-Masonic party, an organization that believed the key to brightening the nation's future was in revealing the secret rules of the Masonic Order, met at the Athenaeum in Baltimore to make a choice. William Wirt was nominated on the first ballot. In the general election the following year (which swept Andrew Jackson into office for a second term), Wirt carried only one state — Vermont.

Although the Anti-Masonic party soon melted away, the concept of political conventions to nominate presidential candidates became one of the most enduring in American politics.

The development of political parties was not the only reason that conventions became popular. Important changes in transportation were taking place. During the 1830s, the number of railroads in the United States multiplied rapidly. By 1835, more than a thousand miles of railroad line with steam-powered locomotives had opened in eleven states. Railroads enabled politicians to get to convention sites safely and efficiently.

In December 1831, the National Republicans, meeting in Baltimore, nominated Henry Clay of Kentucky for President and John Sergeant of Pennsylvania for Vice-President on the first ballot. The following May, the Democratic-Republican party, which also convened in Baltimore, unanimously nominated Jackson for a second term. Martin Van Buren of New York was named the vice-presidential candidate.

During the convention, the Democratic-Republicans adopted

two rulings that were to govern their conventions for a century. One of these was the "two-thirds rule." It stated that in order to be nominated a candidate had to receive two-thirds of the delegate vote, not merely a simple majority.

The convention also adopted the "unit rule," which meant the states were to vote as units, that is, without any recognition of minority votes within a delegation.

In the decades that followed the election of 1832, the importance of national conventions grew enormously. Not only did conventions provide a popular substitute for congressional caucuses, they also helped to establish political parties as organizations that were independent of Congress and state legislatures. Moreover, conventions helped to make the President the leader of his political party as well as the nation's chief executive.

From 1828 through 1856, the Democratic party (the term "Republican" was dropped during the 1830s) dominated American politics, winning six of eight presidential elections. The Democrats did so despite the fact that their members quarreled over several issues of the day, including slavery and tariff rates.

About 1832, several groups (including the National Republicans) that opposed Andrew Jackson joined together to form the Whig party. Although the Whigs managed to elect two Presidents — William Henry Harrison in 1840 and Zachary Taylor in 1848 — the party never matched the Democrats in terms of popular appeal.

The Republican party, the other of the principal political parties of the present day, started as a series of anti-slavery meetings in the Midwest in 1851. At the time, the Whig party was coming apart. Many Whigs, and Northern Democrats as well, opposed the extension of slavery into the territories. On July 6, 1854, at a mass meeting held in Jackson, Michigan, the delegates officially launched a new party, took the name Republican, and adopted a platform that branded slavery "the great moral, social, and political evil" of the day.

As their first presidential candidate, the Republicans chose John C. Frémont, a popular hero, famous for his explorations of the Far West. In the election of 1856, the extension of slavery was the burning issue. Although Frémont carried eleven Northern states, he lost to James Buchanan. The Democratic nominee carried nineteen states, including every southern state except Maryland.

Some sources trace the modern two-party system in the United States to the election of 1856. Since that time, the Democratic and Republican parties have dominated the American political scene. As for conventions, they have come to typify the American political process, and are now looked upon as being as thoroughly American as hot dogs at a baseball game.

CHAPTER THREE

BOSS RULE

For their nominating convention in 1860, the second in Republican history, the party met in the Wigwam, a boxlike, two-story, wooden-frame structure on Lake Street in Chicago. It was the first building constructed especially for a political convention.

The Wigwam offered seating for ten thousand spectators in its huge balconies. Never before had the general public been invited to a presidential nominating convention. The main floor, where there was only standing room, no seating, was reserved for the delegates. The building was decorated with flags, flowers, and evergreens, and fitted out with the latest telegraphic equipment, allowing the hundreds of press representatives who attended the convention to send messages by wire to their respective papers.

Senator William H. Seward of New York, one of the organizers of the Republican party, was favored to win the nomination. A leader of the antislavery forces in Congress, Seward had the financial support of New York State political organizations and had been assured of all but a handful of the 170 votes needed to win the nomination.

The Wigwam Where Abraham Lincoln Was Nominated

The wooden-frame Wigwam, site of the 1860 Republican convention.

One of Seward's rivals was Abraham Lincoln, fifty-one and a newcomer to national politics. Born in Kentucky, raised in Indiana and Illinois, Lincoln had worked as a surveyor and been a captain in the militia during the Black Hawk War. He became a lawyer and went on to serve eight years in the Illinois legislature. Lincoln was elected to Congress in 1846, but his efforts on behalf of the party went unrewarded, and he returned to Springfield, Illinois, to practice law again.

Lincoln wrote to one of his supporters outlining his convention strategy in 1860. "My name is new in the field," he said, "and I suppose I am not the first choice of a great many. Our policy, then, is to give no offense to others—leave them in a mood to come to us if they shall be compelled to give up their first love."

In those days, candidates did not attend conventions but left campaigning to their friends and backers. Lincoln followed this practice, remaining in Springfield, awaiting word of the results.

Lincoln's campaign manager was Judge David Davis. The two men had been lawyers together in Illinois. Weighing close to three hundred pounds, Davis was once described as a "sleepy mountain." But he was quick-witted, shrewd, and hard working.

Davis's strategy was to try to prevent Seward from winning on the first ballot, while at the same time establishing Lincoln as something more than merely a "favorite son" candidate, one who had the backing of his home state and few, if any, others. Once Seward was stalled, Davis hoped to quickly gather support for Lincoln, before the delegates could discover someone else.

As the Republicans poured into Chicago and the day of the balloting drew near, Davis went to work, trading positions in Lincoln's cabinet for delegate votes. Indiana's twenty-six delegates were among the first to be promised to Lincoln. After the election, Indiana's Caleb Smith was named secretary of the interior.

Gideon Welles, who headed the Connecticut delegation, was undecided on how to vote. The Lincoln people met with him. Connecticut's votes went to Lincoln. Welles was later named secretary of the navy.

Davis met with the influential Blair family of Maryland and won the promise that Maryland's votes would swing to Lincoln on the second ballot. Montgomery Blair was given the position of postmaster general.

When the names of the candidates were put into nomination, the cheers of the spectators shook the Wigwam's wooden rafters. But Lincoln got louder cheers than Seward or anyone else. While Seward's followers were parading through the streets of Chicago behind a brass band, Lincoln's backers surged into the Wigwam and filled the spectator seating. And to ensure that Lincoln would be represented on the convention floor with enthusiastic demonstrations, counterfeit tickets were printed and handed out to Lincoln loyalists.

Davis got what he wanted on the first ballot. Seward received 173½ votes, 60 fewer than he required. Lincoln surprised most observers with his strong showing—102 votes. On the second ballot, Lincoln drew closer; it was Seward, 184½, Lincoln, 181. On the third ballot, Davis and his colleagues put Lincoln over the top.

Historians have debated how much trading Davis actually did in

Lincoln's name. Most agree it was a substantial amount. When Davis and his friends told Lincoln the price they had paid for the nomination, Lincoln said, "Well, gentlemen, where do I come in? You seem to have given everything away."

Party Bosses

Such manipulation of convention votes was possible because delegates had no real voice. They were controlled by party bosses, political leaders who dominate state or local party organizations and who manipulate voting and elections. Delegates were frequently party workers who toiled throughout the year on a volunteer basis. As a reward for their efforts, they were given a trip to the convention city that was paid for by the party.

Once on the scene, the delegates relaxed and enjoyed themselves, while the leaders met and negotiated. When it came time to vote, the delegates were instructed whom to vote for.

More than a few conventions of the past resembled the Republican convention of 1860 in that they produced wholly unexpected results. Convention voting would often result in a deadlock, whereupon party leaders would meet and agree upon someone who was virtually unknown — a dark horse.

Speaker of the House James K. Polk, a Democrat from Tennessee, was the first dark-horse candidate. When the roll call was taken for the first ballot at the Democratic convention in 1844, Polk's name was not even mentioned. In fact, not a vote was cast for him during the first seven ballots. The delegates were unable to decide between former President Martin Van Buren and Lewis Cass of Michigan.

On the eighth ballot, Polk's name was introduced as a compromise candidate, and he received 44 votes. Van Buren got 104 votes; Cass, 114. To win the nomination, 177 votes were needed.

On the ninth ballot, the convention suddenly stampeded for Polk. State after state that had supported either Van Buren or Cass switched to him. Before a final tabulation was made, Polk's nomination was made unanimous.

James K. Polk, the first dark-horse candidate, became the eleventh President in 1844.

The Whigs, the principal opposition party of the day, could hardly believe that the Democrats had picked Polk. He was looked upon by some as a ridiculous choice. A jingle of the day went:

> Ha, ha, ha, what a nominee
> Is Jimmy Polk of Tennessee!

Despite the ridicule, Polk went on to defeat Henry Clay in the general election.

In at least one instance, party bosses managed to nominate someone who had no desire to be a candidate. Governor of New York Horatio Seymour, who became the Democratic nominee in 1868, was perhaps the most reluctant candidate in history. Seymour knew that his party's nominee in the 1868 election would be facing General Ulysses S. Grant (who had "saved the Union"), and Seymour had no wish to engage the popular Grant in combat.

The Democratic convention of 1868, held at Tammany Hall in New York City, nominated reluctant candidate Horatio Seymour.

Through twenty-one ballots, Seymour absolutely refused to allow his name to be placed in nomination. But the Democratic bosses became convinced that Seymour represented their best hope. After he had left the meeting hall late one night, his name was placed in nomination. Before the final vote was recorded, the nomination was declared unanimous in his favor. Then the party leaders quickly adjourned the convention so Seymour would not have a chance to turn down the nomination.

When he learned what the convention had done, Seymour is said to have broken down and wept, sobbing to a friend, "Pity me, Harvey, pity me."

There was really no cause for tears. Seymour did well in the election. Although Grant won, his popular majority was only about 310,000 votes (3,021,833 to 2,703,249). However, Grant buried Seymour in the electoral college count, 214 votes to 80.

Theodore Roosevelt, who became the nation's twenty-sixth President in 1901 following the assassination of William McKinley, and won office in his own right in the election of 1904, ran into boss rule when he sought a third term in 1912. His opponent for the Republican nomination that year was President William Howard Taft, whose friends and backers controlled the party machinery. Roosevelt was to learn how tightly they controlled it.

Enormously popular among the voters of the day, Roosevelt rolled to one victory after another in the primaries, winning in Illinois, Pennsylvania, California, Minnesota, Nebraska, Maryland, South Dakota, and New Jersey. He won Taft's home state of Ohio by a margin of almost two to one. Roosevelt lost Massachusetts to the President by a small margin. Robert La Follette, the Progressive leader from Wisconsin, scored victories in his home state and North Dakota.

At the end of the 1912 primary season, the totals looked like this:

CANDIDATE	VOTES
Theodore Roosevelt	1,157,397
William Howard Taft	761,716
Robert La Follette	351,043

While there was no doubt the voters preferred Roosevelt, he had no firm grip on the nomination. The votes of 254 delegates, whose credentials were in question, were being contested. The dispute was to be settled by the Republican National Committee. Unfortunately for Roosevelt, the Committee was controlled by Taft's friends, and it handed 235 of the contested delegates to Taft. Roosevelt received only 19 delegates. To no one's surprise, Taft won the nomination on the first ballot.

Roosevelt's supporters were enraged. They stormed out of the convention and met with their candidate. They cheered when he agreed to run as the head of a third party, the Progressive party. In the general election that fall, the split in the Republican vote allowed the election to be won by Democrat Woodrow Wilson.

When Theodore Roosevelt was denied the Republican nomination in 1912, he and his backers formed a third party, the Progressive party.

The 1920 Republican Convention

The term "smoke-filled room," meaning a room where cigar-smoking party big shots huddle to juggle convention votes and advance someone's candidacy, dates to the 1920 Republican convention in Chicago. The Republicans went to the convention that year without a clear-cut nominee. Among those under consideration, but by no means a favorite, was Senator Warren G. Harding of Ohio.

Harding's candidacy was being promoted by Harry Daugherty, an Ohio lawyer and noted boss of the day. Several months before the convention got underway, Daugherty was asked by a reporter for the *New York Times* how he expected Harding to win the nomination. According to the *Times,* this was Daugherty's answer:

I don't expect Senator Harding to be nominated on the first, second, or third ballots, but I think we can afford to take chances that at about eleven minutes after two, Friday morning of the convention, when twenty or thirty weary men are sitting around the table, someone will say, 'Who will we nominate?' At that decisive time, the friends of Harding will suggest him and we can well afford to abide by the result.

The story was later revised to read "fifteen men, bleary-eyed with lack of sleep and perspiring profusely." Still later, the phrase "in a smoke-filled room" was added.

Despite the revisions, the essential facts remained the same, and the story stands as an amazing bit of forecasting.

After four ballots on Thursday afternoon, none of the front-runners appeared headed for the nomination. A group of Republican leaders, including half a dozen senators, adjourned to a suite of rooms at the Blackstone Hotel. At about two o'clock on Friday morning, legend has it, they sent for Senator Harding for an interview, and they liked his answers to their questions.

At the convention later that day, as the balloting continued, Harding's strength kept building. He was nominated on the tenth ballot, and that fall he scored a decisive victory over Democrat James M. Cox to become the nation's twenty-ninth President.

Support for Primaries Grows

Toward the end of the nineteenth century, a movement for the adoption of presidential primary elections to choose candidates had begun to develop. These elections gave the people a chance to name the person they would like to represent them in the coming election. No longer would the choice of candidates be in the hands of party leaders. "No more boss rule!" was the rallying cry of those who supported the primary process.

Primaries meant that when the delegates from a primary state went to the nominating convention they would know the preference of the people they represented.

STEVENSON FOR PRESIDENT

Adlai Stevenson was the choice of the Democratic party bosses in 1952.

In a speech in 1897, Robert La Follette, later a United States senator from Wisconsin, had argued for the abolition of party caucuses and conventions, which, he said, have "no purpose further than to give respectable form to political robbery." He urged that we "go back to the first principles of democracy, go back to the people. Substitute for both the caucus and the convention a primary election. . . . "

In 1901, Florida adopted an optional primary law, and in 1905 Wisconsin adopted the first state primary election.

Other states passed similar legislation. But it would be many years before primaries would become an effective instrument in selecting candidates for national office. One reason was because many primaries of the early 1900s were merely "advisory" in nature. The voters made known their preferences, but the convention delegates were not mandated to follow them. They continued to vote as the delegation leaders instructed them to vote.

This practice continued until fairly recent times. A candidate could make a strong showing in the primary elections and still be denied the party's nomination at the convention.

In 1952, for instance, Senator Estes Kefauver of Tennessee emerged from the primaries as the most popular Democrat candidate. Yet Illinois Governor Adlai Stevenson walked off with the nomination that year. The reason: the party bosses wanted Stevenson.

Even though John F. Kennedy was active in the primaries in 1960, it was not because he was particularly concerned with the number of votes he might win. Kennedy sought to use the primaries to demonstrate to party bosses that a Catholic candidate could win votes from Protestant voters.

Kennedy's chief rival for the nomination was Minnesota Senator Hubert Humphrey. Humphrey spoke often and at length in support of the full range of liberal programs, including housing and education, social welfare, and civil rights. Senator Lyndon Johnson of Texas was also in the running.

The race came down to key primaries in Wisconsin and West Virginia. Kennedy moved himself, his family, and his campaign staff to Wisconsin for a full month early in 1960, and worked hard there. He sometimes began his day at five-thirty in the morning, visiting dairy farms or shaking hands with factory workers.

Kennedy's hard work paid off, and he won the Wisconsin primary. But some observers said the reason he had won was because many Catholic voters in the state had supported him. The press said Kennedy still needed to prove he could attract broad-based voter support.

West Virginia was the next test. There Kennedy faced an uphill struggle. Certainly he was not going to benefit from any Catholic vote, for West Virginia was 95 percent Protestant. There was much evidence of anti-Catholic feeling, expressed in Sunday sermons and in pamphlets that flooded the state.

Kennedy moved his family and campaign personnel to West Virginia, and worked with the same vigor he had displayed in Wisconsin. He met the religion issue head on. "I am not a Catholic candidate for President," he told voters. "I do not speak for the Catholic church on issues on public policy, and no one in the church speaks for me."

In his speeches and his newspaper and television advertising, Kennedy promoted himself as the candidate of equal opportunity, freedom of religion, and separation of church and state. A vote for Kennedy came to be looked upon as a vote for fairness, while a vote against him came to be thought of as possibly a sign of prejudice.

Many responsible Protestant clergymen said that it was wrong to make a candidate's religion a campaign issue. As for Humphrey, he made it clear he wanted no votes on the basis of religion. Humphrey did, however, express his bitterness at Kennedy's ability to outspend him.

At the beginning, Humphrey was foreseen as the winner in West Virginia. But Kennedy scored an upset victory, winning 61 percent of the vote. Humphrey immediately withdrew from the race and returned to Minnesota to seek reelection to the Senate.

The importance of West Virginia went far beyond the handful of electoral votes that Kennedy could now claim. With his victory there, he demonstrated to party leaders that being rich, young, and

Catholic were not serious drawbacks. He could win voter support.

Party bosses were important on the Republican side, too. Richard Nixon, the party's candidate in 1960, 1968, and again in 1972, and Barry Goldwater, whom the Republicans selected in 1964, won their nominations by working closely with the party leadership. They traveled throughout the country practically the year round, speaking at state party functions and giving assistance to party members. When it came time for a national convention, they pretty much controlled the party apparatus in the various states. Persuading delegates to vote for them was not a difficult matter.

But change was coming. A nominating convention acted out against a background of protest, rage, and violence, and dominated by party bosses who picked a candidate who never bothered to enter the primaries, gave rise to changes that led to the more open and more democratic process the nation enjoys today.

CHAPTER FOUR

CHANGING THE RULES

For the United States, the year 1968 was violent and tragic. On April 4, civil rights leader Martin Luther King, Jr., was killed by an assassin's bullet in Memphis, Tennessee. His death triggered rioting and looting in Washington, D.C. and other cities.

Several weeks later, on June 5, Senator Robert F. Kennedy of New York, brother of the President who had been murdered barely five years before, was shot in Los Angeles, just after he had won the California presidential primary. Kennedy died the next day. The man who pulled the trigger was a young Arab nationalist who was bursting with anger because of Kennedy's friendship with Israel.

All the while, the Vietnam War, in which the United States sought to prevent the North Vietnamese from taking over South Vietnam, was being waged. The war bitterly divided the nation and dominated the contest for the presidency in 1968.

President Lyndon B. Johnson, big, loud, and combative, but also folksy and informal, was the central figure. Johnson, as Vice-President in 1963, had succeeded President Kennedy after his assassination. In winning a term of his own the following year, Johnson had promised voters that he had no intention of sending "American boys 9,000 or 10,000 miles away from home to do what Asian boys ought to be doing for themselves." But Johnson ended up doing exactly that. By 1968, the United States was spending $82 million a day to fight the war in Vietnam, and half a million United States troops were involved there. Nightly news telecasts showed American soldiers falling and dying in the jungles of Southeast Asia. Antiwar and antidraft riots erupted all across America. There were student revolts and a people's march on Washington, with protestors chanting, "Hey, hey, LBJ, how many kids did you kill today?"

Minnesota Senator Eugene McCarthy was the first to challenge President Lyndon B. Johnson for the 1968 Democratic nomination.

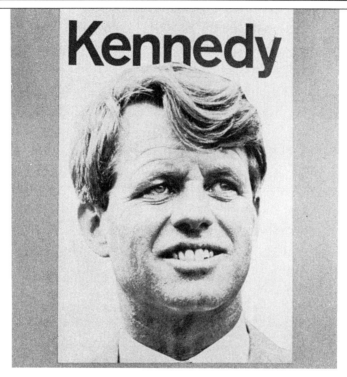

Robert Kennedy also entered the race for the Democratic party's nomination in 1968.

Those who opposed the war at first supported the mild-mannered and bookish Minnesota Senator Eugene McCarthy, who had launched an antiwar campaign for the Democratic nomination in 1967. Early the following year, McCarthy challenged President Johnson by entering the New Hampshire primary, the first of the presidential primaries. McCarthy was a particular favorite of college students, who worked hard on his behalf in New Hampshire. They rang doorbells and made thousands of phone calls in an effort to get McCarthy supporters to the polls.

Although Johnson, a write-in candidate, won the primary with 49.4 percent of the vote, McCarthy captured a surprising 42.4 percent and twenty of the state's twenty-four delegates. The people had spoken; they had made it clear that if Lyndon Johnson wanted to run again for President, he would have a fight on his hands getting his party's nomination.

Robert Kennedy, suddenly realizing Johnson could be beaten, announced he was entering the race. Kennedy declared he wanted "to seek new policies to close the gaps between black and white, rich and poor, young and old in this country and around the world." He had the support of many of his brother's former associates.

Kennedy's awakening was only the beginning. Another result of McCarthy's showing in New Hampshire was President Johnson's announcement that he was withdrawing from the race. He had no desire to oppose the will of the people. "I shall not seek and I will not accept the nomination of my party for another term as your President," said Johnson in his televised speech on March 31, 1968.

Johnson's surprise announcement set the stage for Vice-President Hubert Humphrey to enter the race. Before becoming Vice-President, the amiable Humphrey had been elected to the Senate three times. In the Senate, he was a dedicated leader in the struggle for civil rights, arms control, medical aid to the needy, and aid to education. Unlike his chief rivals for the nomination, Eugene McCarthy and Robert Kennedy, Humphrey made no attempt to separate himself from Johnson's unpopular Vietnam policies.

Meanwhile, primary races were being contested, with McCarthy and Kennedy battling it out state by state. McCarthy won in Wisconsin, in Massachusetts, where Kennedy was a write-in candidate, and in Arizona. Kennedy triumphed in Indiana, Nebraska, and California. After his victory there, and pledging "on to Chicago, and let's win!" Kennedy was assassinated.

Humphrey did not bother to enter the primary contests. Since he and Johnson controlled the Democratic party apparatus, Humphrey could move quietly from state to state, picking up delegates not bound by the outcome of primaries.

A Chaotic Convention

At the Democratic convention in Chicago that summer, Kennedy backers, who might have been expected to support McCarthy and his antiwar candidacy, did not. They were bitter over the campaign that McCarthy had waged in the California primary, where he had

President Lyndon B. Johnson (left) and his Vice-President, Hubert Humphrey, controlled leadership of the Democratic party in the late 1960s.

attacked President John Kennedy for his decision to send American military forces into Vietnam.

Since McCarthy supporters, by themselves, were far too few in number, it was an easy matter for Humphrey to win the nomination on the first ballot. Senator Edmund Muskie of Maine was also quickly approved by the delegates as Humphrey's running mate.

But that was hardly the end of the divisions within the Democratic ranks. There had been heated quarreling between the "hawks," those who supported President Johnson and the war, and the "doves," whose cause was peace, over convention procedures and the platform. The fiercest fight of all was over the platform's Vietnam plank. McCarthy's supporters demanded an immediate halt to the bombings, followed by negotiations for the withdrawal of all foreign troops from South Vietnam. But Humphrey's backers were in control. They got approval for a plank that rejected withdrawal, supported peace talks that were underway in Paris, and called for an end to the bombing, but only "when this action would not endanger the lives of our troops in the field."

DON'T MISS IT!

ATTEND FREE! **GIGANTIC! FANTASTIC!**

TEXAS WANTS HUMPHREY RALLY

SUNDAY, NOVEMBER 3 - 3 P. M. - ASTRODOME

See! Hear! VICE-PRESIDENT **HUBERT HUMPHREY**

Be entertained by **FRANK SINATRA** and 40-pc. orchestra

also Nancy Sinatra, Trini Lopez, Edie Adams, The Blossoms, Flags, Patriotism, Fun!

GATES OPEN 1 PM !

In the 1968 campaign for the presidency, Humphrey drew close to Nixon but could not overtake him.

The struggle between the hawks and the doves was also played out on the streets of Chicago. A huge army of protestors converged upon the city in the days before the convention. Among them were peace activitists, mostly young people who rejected war in principle. Many of the protestors had been active in campaigning for McCarthy or Kennedy and now thought the Democrats were going to nominate Hubert Humphrey. Such a turn of events would be unfair and illegitimate, they believed.

The protestors also included thousands of hippies, young people who rejected many of the standards and customs of the day and political organizations in particular. They were on hand mostly to mock and jeer at the system. Chicago's Mayor Richard Daley was prepared for them. "No one," he declared, "is going to take over the streets." He ordered the city's entire police force to stand twelve-hour shifts and arranged for thousands of National Guard and army troops to be mobilized. Chicago was like a war zone.

The week of the convention, there were minor, although at times bloody, disputes between the police and demonstrators. But the night that Humphrey was nominated, a major battle broke out. When the demonstrators sought to march to the International Amphitheatre, where the convention was being held, the police charged into them, attacking with clubs and tear gas. A stunned nation watched the chaos on television. Scenes of the riot were also shown on a giant television screen inside the amphitheatre.

Although Humphrey won the Democratic party's endorsement that night, he had no sense of triumph or joy. "My wife and I went home heartbroken," Humphrey later told Theodore White, author of *The Making of the President 1968*. "I told her I felt like we had just been in a shipwreck."

In the election campaign that fall, Humphrey faced Richard Nixon, making a comeback after having been defeated by John F. Kennedy in 1960. Nixon began far ahead of Humphrey in the public opinion polls. He could also boast of a united party and plenty of money. Humphrey could make no such claims.

Almost everywhere he went, Humphrey was taunted by hecklers who looked upon him as representing President Johnson's Vietnam policies. "Stop the war!" protestors chanted when Humphrey sought to speak. Other times he heard, "Dump the Hump! Dump the Hump!"

Toward the end of the campaign, Humphrey began to put some distance between himself and President Johnson. He even called for a halt in the bombing of North Vietnam. As Election Day neared, Humphrey was becoming the "peace" candidate. Eugene McCarthy endorsed him.

In the election, the popular vote was close, Nixon winning by only 510,314 votes (31,785,480 to 31,275,166). In the electoral college, however, Nixon won by a big margin, 301 votes to 191 votes.

The election loss served to increase the resentment of those Democrats who had opposed the Vietnam War, President Johnson, and Hubert Humphrey, whom they saw as Johnson's puppet. They continued to charge that party bosses had "stolen" the nomination from Eugene McCarthy and handed it to Humphrey.

The Democrats Make Changes

The Democratic leadership responded to the charges. Between 1968 and 1972, the Democrats wrote new rules governing the selection of delegates and the conduct of presidential primaries. The new rules were meant to soothe those who felt most victimized by all that had taken place in Chicago.

The new rules gave greater representation to women's rights activists, social justice seekers, and civil rights workers. The rules made it mandatory that blacks, women, and young people be given greater representation as state delegates. They required that "affirmative steps" be taken by state parties to ensure that each group's share of delegate slots bear a "reasonable relationship to the group's presence in the population of the state."

Another change the Democrats made was to ban unit rule, the "winner-take-all" rule that had prevailed in the primaries. Under unit rule, a state delegation's entire vote had to be cast for the candidate preferred by the majority of delegates. Republicans had never used unit rule, which was introduced by the Democrats in 1860.

Winner-take-all primaries were replaced with proportional primaries. Each candidate would receive a number of delegates that was in direct proportion to the number of votes he or she received.

In the future, proportional voting would help the little-known or underdog candidate. Whatever support he or she received would be reflected in the delegate count.

Another rule that went into effect in time for the 1972 convention stated that delegates to the national convention had to be chosen in the year of the convention, rather than at some earlier date. This, too, was to cause candidates to revise their strategy. Before, candidates waited until state parties had chosen their convention delegates, and then sought to win their support. But with the new rule, candidates did not wait for delegates to be chosen. Instead, they tried to get their supporters chosen as delegates.

Yet another rule change had to do with "advisory" primaries. These were primaries in which voters selected one candidate over another, but the delegates were not held to the voters' choice. Advisory primaries were mere popularity contests. Delegates were free agents, voting almost as they wished or according to the will of the state party chairperson. But after 1968, delegates were made to reflect the wishes of the voters in their selection of candidates.

While the Republicans sought to end discrimination in party ranks and broaden party membership, they did not feel pressure to change the nominating process as deeply as the Democrats had done. Reforms made by the Republicans were much less drastic.

Once the new rules took effect, the whole system of winning the Democratic nomination changed drastically. It became possible for a relatively small number of activists to rally around a candidate, and by appealing directly to primary and caucus voters, start the candidate on the road to the nomination.

Being a party regular after 1968 was no longer as important as it once had been. Knowing the party leaders was not required. The individual seeking the nomination could go directly to the voters by using the media to become known. Not since Andrew Jackson's day and the switch from congressional caucuses to conventions had the political process experienced such startling change.

The individual who served as chairman of the commission that rewrote the Democratic party rules to take control of the nominating process away from party regulars and put it in the hands of ordinary voters was Senator George McGovern of South Dakota. McGovern also had made an attempt to win the Democratic nomination in 1968 and lost to Hubert Humphrey.

McGovern was very much the dark horse in 1968. Only a handful of people had ever heard of him at the time he announced his candidacy. A former history and political science teacher at Dakota Wesleyan University, McGovern had served two terms in the House of Representatives and had been a minor official in John Kennedy's administration. In 1962, he became the first Democrat in twenty-six years to win election to the Senate from South Dakota.

George McGovern was reelected to the Senate in 1968, the year he first sought the Democratic nomination. During the early 1970s, he emerged as the chief spokesperson for antiwar activists, women's rights organizations, and social-justice workers. These groups comprised McGovern's base as he sought the 1972 Democratic nomination.

George McGovern's 1972 campaign literature featured a peace symbol and a confident "thumbs up" sign.

McGovern was the underdog. The leading Democrat in all the polls was Edmund Muskie, a senator from the state of Maine. Muskie pursued the nomination in the traditional manner, by securing endorsements from party leaders, from senators, from members of the House, governors, and mayors. But by the time Muskie got around to making a formal announcement of his candidacy, McGovern was well on his way to winning the nomination.

McGovern won the Democratic nomination because he had gone out and gotten the support of many thousands of hard-working, grass-roots activists. He led his hordes of young volunteers on an assault on the state conventions and primaries and took them over from the party regulars. When McGovern arrived at Miami Beach, where the Democrats held their convention in 1972, he had all the delegates he needed. Party professionals, such as Chicago's Mayor Daley, did not even bother to show up. McGovern was nominated on the first ballot.

"My nomination is all the more precious," said McGovern in his acceptance speech, "in that it is a gift of the most open political process in history."

George McGovern had perceived that it was a new ballgame. And he had demonstrated to presidential candidates of the future how the game was to be won.

CHAPTER FIVE

THE CANDIDATE AND THE PARTY

To be a successful candidate today, it's important to be a media star. A man or woman who hopes to win any political race, from mayor to President, has to be telegenic, that is, make a pleasing appearance on television. Through the television and the press, it's possible for a candidate to capture a mass following and become a popular leader.

The candidate also needs money, a lot of money. He or she also requires a smooth-working campaign organization.

However, political parties still play a key role in determining who reaches the top. No candidate can win an election by himself or herself. The candidate must get the backing of party leaders and the general membership—the "rank and file." Only on rare occasions has a candidate won a party's presidential nomination without being the choice of the majority of the party's members. The last time it happened was in 1952, when Governor Adlai E. Stevenson of Illinois was nominated by the Democrats over Senator Estes Kefauver of Tennessee.

Lenora Fulani represented the New Alliance party in the 1988 presidential election. It was the only minor party to be on the ballot in all fifty states.

Stevenson trailed Kefauver in a preconvention poll of the party's rank and file.

From 1860 until the present time, the great party rivals in the United States have been the Democrats and Republicans. Third parties, also called minor parties, sometimes offer serious competition. But while third parties have often enlivened campaigns, one has yet to produce a presidential winner. In 1988, minor-party presidential candidates included Ron Paul of the Libertarian party and Lenora Fulani of the New Alliance party. These and other third-party candidates accounted for less than 1 percent of the more than 90 million votes cast in the November election in which Republican George Bush defeated Democrat Michael Dukakis.

Party Organization

The major political parties in the United States are complicated organizations. Both the Democrats and Republicans are organized at the national, state, and local levels.

The smallest local unit is the precinct. There are more than 146,000 election precincts in the United States. The precinct workers, often volunteers, are the people who solicit votes by ringing doorbells or making telephone calls during election campaigns. They are the party's closest link to the voters.

Each precinct is represented on the party's county committee, the next step up the ladder in party organization. The county committee elects the county chairperson, whose job it is to know the voting patterns of each of the county's precincts and get party candidates elected. The county chairperson also keeps in touch with the state party organization.

It is the fifty state organizations, each of which operates as an independent unit, that carry the heaviest load when it comes to running the party. There is a good reason for this: the Constitution mandates that each state is to make its own election laws.

There is another reason for the importance of the party's state organization. In every presidential election, the states play a crucial role when the vote is counted.

Many voters do not realize it, but when they cast their ballots, they are not voting directly for the President and Vice-President. They are actually voting for presidential electors from their states.

Each state has a certain number of electors, which is the total of the state's senators and representatives in Congress. In the presidential election of 1988, California and New York had the most electoral votes. California had forty-seven; New York had thirty-six. Alaska, Delaware, North Dakota, South Dakota, Vermont, and Wyoming each had three electoral votes, as did the District of Columbia.

On Election Day, the candidate who gets the highest number of popular votes in every state except Maine gets all of that state's electoral votes. The District of Columbia also gives its three electoral votes to the overall winner. For example, in 1988 the popular vote in Texas was as follows:

CANDIDATE	**NUMBER OF POPULAR VOTES**
George Bush	3,014,607
Michael Dukakis	2,331,286

Since Bush got more popular votes than Dukakis, he got all twenty-nine of Texas's electoral votes. Dukakis got no electoral votes in Texas.

The state of Maine, with four electoral votes, awarded two electors to the statewide winner and one to the winner in each of the state's two congressional districts.

In 1988, there were a total of 538 electoral votes. There were 435 members of the House of Representatives (a variable number) and 100 senators (a constant number). The District of Columbia had 3 electoral votes, equivalent to two senators and one representative. The candidate who gets a majority of electoral votes is the winner.

The system of electors gives the states enormous importance in presidential elections. Both the Democrats and the Republicans have organizations in each state. The men and women who run these organizations—called state committees—are frequently the most powerful figures in the party. They usually have had experience on the precinct and county levels. Once they have assumed leadership responsibilities on a state level, heads of the party organization devote almost all of their time to the job. They raise campaign money and direct statewide election campaigns. They know the voters in their states and, most importantly, know what kind of candidates will attract votes.

The entire party organization is tied together by the national committee, which is made up of members of state parties. Both the Democratic and Republican National Committees have their headquarters in Washington, D.C.

Political Activists and Political Parties

Americans of voting age vary enormously in the amount of interest they have in presidential elections. When a campaign is

The Reverend Jesse Jackson speaks at a voter registration rally
in New York City in 1988.

underway, most voters are content to follow the unfolding of events on the evening news telecast. They often make their voting decisions on the basis of information that has been provided by the nightly network and local newscasters.

Sometimes, however, specific issues stir the ordinary voter. Talk of a big tax increase, a period of runaway inflation, or a sharp rise in the unemployment rate—any of these can trigger an increase in voter interest.

Some voters are always deeply aware of political issues and events. They have a personal stake in public policy and care deeply about who holds public office.

Who are these people? They are public officials and civil-service employees, that is, individuals whose jobs require deep-seated political interest. A school teacher, for example, is usually concerned about elections for the local board of education or for the city council.

Others who have more than a passing interest in political matters are members of racial or ethnic minorities. Issues concerning blacks, Hispanics, or Asians can make members of these groups politically active. They might be eager, for example, to support an appeal for affirmative action, that is, laws that would help provide equal opportunity in employment or college admissions.

Activists devote more time and energy to political matters than do ordinary citizens. They read books and magazine articles about political topics and government. They attend meetings where political topics are discussed, and they see to it that their views are heard. They make themselves and their views known to public officials. Activists are likely to join political parties and work on behalf of party candidates. They are much more likely to vote in primaries and take part in caucuses than ordinary voters.

Regional issues often cause people to become political activists. In Iowa, Kansas, Nebraska, and other midwestern states, farmers are frequently the political activists. In Texas, for example, those who explore for, drill for, and sell oil often become politically active. In the west, political activists are often those people who are concerned about the conservation of wilderness areas.

In the Democratic party, activists tend to be liberal. In the Republican party, they tend to be conservative.

Conservatives are generally traditionalists. They want to preserve the best of the past and make sure it continues into the future. They believe that too much "big government" can be harmful to democracy. In the recent past of the United States, conservatives have campaigned against high taxes, excessive government regulation, and big spending programs.

Liberals, on the other hand, expect the federal government to play an active role in solving social problems. Liberals generally support such social programs as unemployment insurance, national health insurance, minimum-wage laws, old-age pensions, and anti-poverty legislation.

Certain parts of the country are considered liberal strongholds, while conservatives predominate in other areas. The Northeast is usually defined by political experts as the most liberal part of the country. The South is generally viewed as conservative.

While most Republicans are conservative to moderate, and most Democrats are moderate to liberal, present-day political figures seldom conform exactly to liberal or conservative labels. There is a wide range of thought and belief within each party. Candidates for the presidential nomination of their party must win the support of one wing of the party without exciting too much opposition from the other factions.

In the 1988 presidential election, Michael Dukakis, the Democratic candidate, was considered a liberal in the traditional sense, as was Jesse Jackson, his chief rival. However, Jackson Democrats were regarded as being more liberal than Dukakis Democrats. They were also younger.

New York Governor Mario Cuomo, a Democrat, was sometimes called an "old liberal" in the 1980s. The label had nothing to do with his age. He earned the tag as a result of his vigorous defense of help for the poor and of social equality in an electrifying speech before the Democratic convention in 1984.

Similar variations were seen among the Republicans in the late 1980s. Ronald Reagan appealed the most to Republicans who

	1988 Presidential Primary — New York COL 1 Democratic	1988 Presidential Primary — New York COL 2 Democratic	1988 Presidential Primary — New York COL 3 Democratic	1988 Presidential Primary — New York COL 4 Democratic	1988 Presidential Primary — New York COL 5 Democratic	1988 Presidential Primary — New York COL 6 Democratic	1988 Presidential Primary — New York COL 7 Democratic
President of the United States Presidente de los Estados Unidos Vote for one—Vote por uno	Jesse L. Jackson	Albert Gore, Jr.	Michael S. Dukakis	Paul Simon	Uncommitted	Lyndon H. LaRouche, Jr.	Richard A. Gephardt
Delegates to National Convention Vote for any Five Delegados a la Convencion Nacional Vote por Cinco	Dennis H. Rivera (M)	Stuart Appelbaum (M)	Alexander B. Grannis (M)	Carolyn B. Maloney (F)			
	Margaret Stewart (F)	Jane Huntley (F)	Carol Greitzer (F)	Philip Wachtel (M)			
	Edwin Ortiz, Jr. (M)	Gregory L. Lambert (M)	George A. Hirsch (M)	Joyce D. Miller (F)			
	Anne M. Emerman (F)	Barbara G. Whitney (F)	Sandra Feldman (F)	Kenneth A. Mills (M)			
	Waverly Howard (M)	David Mark Gilbert (M)	Arnold S. Lehman (M)	Nancy B. Siegel (F)			
	Roberto P. Caballero (M)						
	Nora H. Lugo (F)						
	Leo Lawrence (M)						
	May Ying Chen (F)						
	Raymond L. Riccio (M)						
	George N. Spitz (M)						
	Karen M. Lantz (F)						
	Joseph I. Sellman (M)						
	Norma Rogers (F)						
	Joseph J. Williams (M)						
Alternate Delegates to National Convention Vote for any Two Delegados Alternos a la Convencion Nacional Vote por Dos	Bonnie Potter (F)	Jo Ann Bing (F)	Peter Joseph Philip (M)	Sylvia M. Friedman (F)			
	John Curtis (M)		Trudy L. Mason (F)	Richard Dresselhuys (M)			
	Socorro Rentas (F)						
	Leroy T. Corbin (M)						

The ballot used in the Democratic party's presidential primary in New York State in 1988.

called themselves conservatives. Reverend Pat Robertson and Representative Jack Kemp, who were early contenders in the race for the nomination in 1988, shared some of Reagan's views. George Bush's supporters, however, did not think of themselves or their candidate as conservative; they were more "moderate" in their views.

The Issues and Political Parties

Party members are concerned not only about a candidate's political ideology and personal vision; they also want to know his or her positions on matters of public concern—the issues. What does the candidate have to say about such domestic matters as the Equal Rights Amendment, day care for children, Social Security reform, the minimum wage, and health care?

*President Ronald Reagan appealed to the conservative wing
of the Republican party.*

Some candidates pick out a particular issue or cause and seek to be identified with it. In 1988, for example, Democratic candidate Jesse Jackson sought to win the support of workers and farmers with an economic message tailored for these groups. Jack Kemp stressed an anti-Communist foreign policy in his quest for the Republican nomination. George Bush won the Republican nomination by simply promising to continue Ronald Reagan's domestic and foreign policies.

Of course, voters choose one candidate over another for reasons besides the issues of the day. A voter may be swayed on the basis of a candidate's "image" or personal appeal. Another voter may follow the advice of a friend or relative. Race, ethnic background, and religion can also be factors.

Once a candidate has won the support of the party's leaders and its rank and file, the next step is to get the party's nomination. There may be other candidates from the same party who want the same job. They run against each other in primary elections, with the winner going on to the general election.

CHAPTER SIX

GETTING READY

To win a party's presidential nomination today, primaries are the key. What exactly is a primary? It is a preliminary election in which members of a party in a state vote to choose a candidate *and/or* select some or all of a state party organization's delegates to the national convention.

The following statistics indicate how important primaries have become. In 1968, only seventeen states selected delegates to the national convention by means of primaries. By 1988, the number of states using primaries had almost doubled, climbing to thirty-three.

In 1968, only 36.7 percent of the delegates were chosen by primaries. By 1988, the number had grown to almost 65 percent.

The first primaries are held in February of the election year, and the primary season continues for the next five or six months. But long before then — indeed *years* before — the candidate starts planning his or her campaign. Hiring a staff is one of the first steps. A candidate needs a campaign manager, fund-raisers, delegate experts, pollsters, media specialists, and other political advisors.

Without a skilled and experienced staff, a candidate cannot hope to be successful. In 1988, George Bush assembled a team made up of men and women who were tried and proven in presidential campaigns. They were the best talent the Republican party had to offer. The *New York Times* described Bush's staff as ". . . an extraordinarily seasoned crew of communications experts."

The Republican team was in sharp contrast to the staff put together by Bush's opponent, Governor Michael Dukakis of Massachusetts. Dukakis relied largely on men and women who had served him while governor. They had the management experience that helped to make Dukakis the best-financed and best-organized candidate in the race for the Democratic nomination. But in the fall campaign, which is largely a war of communications waged on television and in the press, Dukakis was overmatched. "The long and the short of it is, the Bush campaign ran a better campaign than we did," said Kirk O'Donnell, a senior adviser to Dukakis, shortly after the election results were in.

Republican candidates of the 1980s also benefited from the fact that they could choose from a pool of staff members who had previously worked in winning campaigns or in the White House. From 1968 up to and including George Bush's election victory in 1988, the Democrats posted only one national election win: in 1976 with Jimmy Carter. Democratic staffers who knew the taste of victory were somewhat rare.

Needed: Money

People are not the only part of a successful campaign. Money is vital. No candidate has the slightest chance of succeeding without many millions of dollars.

In 1988, the Democratic and Republican nominations went to the candidates who raised the most money, raised it in time for the first caucuses and primaries, and spent it wisely.

Money buys a skilled and experienced campaign director, advisers and consultants, pollsters, and people to raise more money. It buys advertising, particularly expensive television advertising. It buys buttons, bumper stickers, fliers, brochures, posters, and the hundreds of other items a campaign requires.

And, remember, the money raised by a presidential candidate is not just spent in one state or a handful of states. Campaigns have to be funded in each of the thirty or forty states where primaries and caucuses are held.

Beginning in 1988, big chunks of money went toward purchasing computer systems. Some candidates, such as Senator Robert J. Dole of Kansas, a Republican, had expensive and powerful minicomputers with a full staff to run them. Others, such as Representative Richard A. Gephart of Missouri, a Democrat, used a standard personal computer.

"It's really mind boggling, the difference computers are making this year," Norman Watts, Dole's national political director, told the *Washington Post* in 1988. "A few years ago, we were lucky to have an electronic calculator to collect and analyze precinct numbers."

Dole's computer system kept track of his schedule, his speeches, his opponents, the polls, plus the names of voters, contributors, and volunteers. In previous campaigns, much of this information had been kept on three-by-five cards. Each card had to be painstakingly updated by hand. For a major campaign, a computer "is absolutely necessary to be equipped for battle," said Norman Watts.

Computer systems are not cheap. Michael Conlin, a computer consultant to the Republican party, estimated that of the more than $2 billion that was spent on the presidential, congressional, and other campaigns in 1988, between 15 and 25 percent went to computer services and their related campaign weapon, direct mail. This is advertising that normally consists of letters or brochures that appeal for one's vote or financial support. Direct mail is an efficient way to reach voters. No American household escapes.

Money is also important because it helps a candidate stay in the race after a defeat or two. In 1988, Michael Dukakis's quest for the Democratic nomination was jolted by a primary defeat in Illinois and a caucus defeat in Michigan. But Dukakis, who had raised more money than any of his Democratic rivals, was able to keep his campaign rolling along.

Raising Money

The methods of raising campaign money have changed drastically in recent years. Funds used to be raised by each candidate's own finance committees, which in turn received contributions from special committees in the states.

This system led to serious abuses. Fund-raisers for Richard Nixon's 1972 campaign accepted a $200,000 contribution from financier Robert Vesco, who was seeking to avoid prosecution in an investigation that was being conducted by the Justice Department. The dairy industry also donated $2 million to Nixon's 1972 campaign. In return, an increase in milk prices was promised by the Nixon administration.

There were even more serious abuses, too. On June 17, 1972, not long before Nixon was nominated by the Republican party, a group of men was arrested for breaking into the headquarters of the Democratic National Committee, then located at the Watergate apartment and office building complex in Washington, D.C. When caught, the burglars were photographing documents in the files of the Democrats.

It was soon discovered that one of the burglars was James W. McCord, the security coordinator for the Committee for the Re-election of the President (CRP). The burglars, hired by CRP, had broken into the same offices several weeks before to plant bugging equipment in the Democrats' telephones.

When the burglars were taken into custody, it was found they had in their possession a large supply of $100 bills. The money was later traced to contributions given CRP to pay for campaign expenses. The use of campaign funds to finance a burglary shocked the country.

As the Watergate investigation continued, other illegal acts involving large sums of cash were revealed. Some of the money had been contributed by party members or backers who sincerely believed that Richard Nixon deserved a second term as President. But other big sums came from individual business leaders or corporations who were seeking special favors from Nixon or his advisers.

The Committee for the Reelection of the President raised more money than any other political organization in American history. Much of it was in cash that had never been reported, as was required by law.

Nixon was an overwhelming winner in the 1972 election. Not only was he reelected by 60.8 percent of the popular vote, he also carried forty-nine states with 520 electoral votes. McGovern managed to carry only 37.5 percent of the popular vote and only Massachusetts and the District of Columbia with 17 electoral votes.

The Watergate investigation continued after the election. Grand juries, investigative reporters, and congressional committees unraveled what proved to be one of the biggest political scandals in American history. In the end, seven officials of the Nixon administration or members of his 1972 reelection committee were indicted on charges of conspiracy in attempting to cover up the Watergate break-in. Nixon himself, facing impeachment by the House of Representatives, resigned as President on August 8, 1974. Less than two years before, he had achieved one of the most stunning election victories of all time. Vice-President Gerald R. Ford took office the same day Nixon resigned.

Reforms in Financing Campaigns

The Watergate scandal led Congress to approve widespread reforms in the financing of federal election campaigns. Beginning with the election of 1976, the new laws set limits on the size of campaign contributions and expenses. More important, the legislation provided money to pay campaign costs.

According to the new law, to qualify for federal funds to finance a primary campaign, a candidate must raise at least $5,000 in each of twenty states in amounts of no more than $1,000 per contribution. Once this is done, the federal government will match whatever funds the candidate has raised, up to a specific limit. The limit was $6.6 million in 1988.

Federal funds are available to any individual who aspires to be President, provided, of course, the person meets the qualifications mandated by the Constitution. It doesn't matter whether he or she

The Watergate scandal involved a greater number of high-level government officials than any other previous political scandal.

Form **1040**	Department of the Treasury—Internal Revenue Service **U.S. Individual Income Tax Return**	19**88** (O)		
	For the year Jan.–Dec. 31, 1988, or other tax year beginning , 1988, ending , 19			OMB No. 1545-0074
Label Use IRS label. Otherwise, please print or type.	L A B E L H E R E	Your first name and initial (if joint return, also give spouse's name and initial) Last name		Your social security number
		Present home address (number, street, and apt. no. or rural route). (If a P.O. Box, see page 6 of Instructions.)		Spouse's social security number
		City, town or post office, state, and ZIP code		For Privacy Act and Paperwork Reduction Act Notice, see Instruction
Presidential Election Campaign ▶	Do you want $1 to go to this fund?		Yes ▨ No	**Note:** *Checking "Yes" will not change your tax or reduce your refund.*
	If joint return, does your spouse want $1 to go to this fund?. .		Yes ▨ No	

Federal Income Tax Form No. 1040 enables a taxpayer to indicate whether he or she wishes to contribute $1 to a presidential election campaign fund.

is a Democrat, Republican, or member of a third party. However, minor party candidates are not eligible for the same amounts as those representing major parties.

If a candidate does not want to accept federal matching funds, no limit is placed on the amount he or she may spend on the campaign. The individual can spend as much money as can be raised.

Where does the money come from? From the taxpayers, of course. In a box on the federal income tax return, a taxpayer can indicate whether one dollar of his or her payment should go into the fund to match the money raised by the presidential candidates. This means that for every dollar the candidates raise, the government will contribute a dollar. In return, the candidates agree to spending limits.

Announcing the Candidacy

Once a candidate has assembled a staff and begun raising money, an early and important move is to announce his or her candidacy. This used to be a rather simple matter. The presidential hopeful would walk into the rotunda of a state capitol building or a Senate caucus room and declare the race was on.

Television changed that. An announcement now presents an opportunity for television and press coverage — "free media" — as the candidates call it. It's an opportunity few candidates want to pass up.

Some candidates try to make announcement day as exciting as possible, thereby hoping to attract the maximum amount of television and press coverage. In April 1987, when former Secretary of State Alexander M. Haig announced he would be seeking the Republican presidential nomination, he did it at the posh Waldorf Astoria Hotel in New York. Comedian Mort Sahl and Peter Duchin's orchestra performed for the occasion.

When Governor Michael Dukakis of Massachusetts announced early in 1987 that he would be pursuing the Democratic presidential nomination, he tried a different strategy—the "fly around." He made his announcement in Boston, then hopped a plane and raced off to New Hampshire, Iowa, and other points to repeat the announcement. Iowa and New Hampshire are key states. Early caucuses (in February in 1988) are held in Iowa. New Hampshire offers the first primary test. Getting local stations to cover the announcement in those states is deemed as important as getting network news coverage.

Sometimes a presidential hopeful, instead of making a clearcut announcement, will hold a press conference to announce that sometime in the future there is going to be an announcement. This can happen when speculation is building about the contender's candidacy and the hopeful wants to put an end to that speculation. Yet the candidate is not quite ready to make a formal announcement. Of course, the intentions of some hopefuls are so well known that preannouncements are hardly necessary. Everyone knows the race is already being run. Candidates in this category have included George Bush and Jesse Jackson.

The Preseason

The period just after the candidate makes his or her announcement but before the primaries and caucuses begin is almost as important as the primaries and caucuses themselves. This period is called the "preseason."

During the preseason, each candidate must work hard to be taken seriously by the media. This is not a problem for someone such as

George Bush, for example, who served two terms as Vice-President before he launched his campaign for the 1988 Republican nomination. But former Delaware Governor Pierre Samuel (Pete) du Pont or television evangelist Pat Robertson, who were among Bush's early rivals, had difficulty making themselves credible candidates. Each often heard himself described as a long shot or even "an extremely long shot" candidate.

The media watches carefully to see whom the candidates hire as staff members. Those who choose managers, pollsters, and fundraisers who are skilled and respected in their fields gain stature. Without top help, it's difficult for a candidate to appear serious.

The preseason of the 1988 election campaign was the most intensive in history. There were seven, sometimes eight, Democratic candidates, individuals with solid records but whose reputations were largely regional. The Republicans offered five candidates, including two well-known figures, Vice-President Bush and Senate Minority Leader Robert J. Dole of Kansas.

These candidates met in a series of televised debates. But, as Senator Paul Simon of Illinois, a Democratic candidate that year, pointed out, "debate" was really the wrong word to use in describing the multicandidate encounters. In 1858, Abraham Lincoln, campaigning against Stephen A. Douglas for a Senate seat in Illinois, faced his opponent in a series of debates in each of the state's seven congressional districts. To Simon, these were "real" debates. Lincoln asked questions of Douglas, and Douglas posed questions for Lincoln. There were no journalists involved. "The debates of the 1988 primary campaign," said Simon, "were as different from the Lincoln-Douglas debates as a Beethoven symphony is from a radio jingle."

In 1988 journalists asked the questions. Each candidate's reply had to be kept to a minute or less. This enabled candidates to avoid direct answers. In one debate, for example, former Secretary of State Alexander M. Haig, Jr., himself a candidate, asked George Bush what he had done about the Iran-Contra arms deal. Two former aides to President Reagan were among those indicted in 1988 in connection with the sale of weapons to Iran and the transfer of profits to the Contras, who were fighting the Sandinista regime in Nicaragua.

Haig tried to find out how deeply Bush might have been involved. "Were you in the cockpit," Haig asked, "or were you on an economy ride in the back of the plane?"

Bush dodged the question, saying the Reagan administration had attempted to correct the mistakes the Iran-Contra affair had brought to light. When Haig asked for an example, Bush grinned and said, "Time's up."

The Democrats held twenty debates, the Republicans, fourteen. While the debates forced the news media to focus on where the candidates stood on various issues and also on their skills as television performers, that is, their style and mannerisms, the debates decided little. At the end of the preseason, the Democratic candidates were still tightly packed. The Republican situation had been made somewhat clearer, however, with Bush and Dole drawing away from the other candidates.

Lee Atwater, Bush's campaign manager, felt the 1988 debates were not of great importance. "I'm convinced the public loses interest after the first debate," he said.

Larry Sabato, a professor of government at the University of Virginia, had mixed feelings about the debates. "On the one hand, there are more opportunities for people to learn about politics," he told the *New York Times*. "On the other hand, the fact that we do have a permanent campaign may stifle interest."

CHAPTER SEVEN

THE ROAD TO VICTORY

The obvious reason primaries are important to a candidate is that they supply delegates to the national convention. The candidate who commands a majority of delegates wins the party's nomination.

But primaries have other values. As the election season unfolds, primary victories can demonstrate a candidate's popularity. By winning primaries, a candidate's campaign grows in importance. Greater media coverage and a higher ranking in the polls are certain to result. The candidate has an easier time raising funds and attracting volunteer workers.

Rules and regulations governing primaries are set by state law, state party organizations, and the Democratic and Republican National Committees. Most primaries are "closed." This means that voting is limited to members of a particular party. Some states, however, have "open primaries." An open primary is one in which all voters, whether or not they are registered with a particular party, are eligible to vote. In 1988, Alabama, Georgia, Missouri, North Carolina, Tennessee, and Virginia were among the states that offered open primaries.

States design the primary ballots, and this can cause some problems. In 1988, in its effort to make the arrangement of names on the ballots as fair as possible, the state of Pennsylvania produced a ballot that bewildered voters.

The delegate names on the ballot were not grouped by candidate. Instead, they were scattered all around the ballot. Inside the voting booth, a voter had to first flip a lever beside the name of his or her choice for the party's presidential nomination and then sift through the names, choosing each of the candidate's delegates. "You need a road map to vote," said one delegate.

Michael Dukakis, the Democratic candidate, spent thousands of dollars on radio commercials to explain the ballot to his supporters. "On April 26 in the Pennsylvania primary," said one commercial, "one vote for Mike Dukakis won't be enough. If you want to help send Mike to the White House, you've got to vote for all the Dukakis delegates in our area."

Fliers were distributed to go along with the radio campaign. "In the Second Congressional District," said one flier, "vote twelve times for Dukakis."

Some states prefer caucuses instead of presidential primaries. A caucus is a meeting of party members, and any voter registered with that party may attend.

At a caucus, each party member gets one vote. In some states, the individual party member votes for the person he or she thinks should be the candidate. In other states, each party member votes for a delegate or a slate of delegates to the state convention. The party member knows that the person or persons sent to the convention will support his or her choice.

The first caucuses and primaries are held during January and February of the election year. The quest for delegates continues until June. In 1988, Democratic candidates competed for a total of 4,163 delegate votes (with 2,082 votes required to win the nomination). For Republican candidates, 2,277 delegate votes were available (with 1,139 needed to win).

DIXVILLE NOTCH, NEW HAMPSHIRE 1988 PRESIDENTIAL PRIMARY			
DEMOCRATIC		REPUBLICAN	
PAUL SIMON	3	JACK KEMP	5
BRUCE BABBITT		PAT ROBERTSON	1
MICHAEL S. DUKAKIS		GEORGE BUSH	11
DICK GEPHARDT	4	BOB DOLE	6
AL GORE		PETE DU PONT	2
GARY HART		ALEXANDER M. HAIG	2
JESSE JACKSON			

New Hampshire is the first state to hold a presidential primary. The town of Dixville Notch is traditionally the first to report returns.

New Hampshire is the first state to hold a primary election, and in years to come it will continue to be. State law in New Hampshire says that its primary must take place before any other state's.

New Hampshire is a small state. Its total population is about the same as that of the cities of Dallas, Texas, or Phoenix, Arizona. Most of New Hampshire's approximately 110,000 Democrats live in the state's southern half. Candidates can practice "retail politics" in New Hampshire. That is, they can talk to voters personally, visiting barber shops and supermarkets, shoe factories and high-tech electronic plants, offices and schools.

"Super Tuesday"

The second Tuesday in March is one of the most important dates on the primary calendar. "Super Tuesday" marks a huge regional primary. Some have even called it a "megaprimary." In 1988, twenty states, half of them in the South, held primaries or caucuses on Super Tuesday, with voters selecting 1,307 Democratic delegates (31.4 percent of the total) and 803 Republican delegates (35.2 percent of the total).

The Democratic state legislatures in the South planned Super Tuesday with the hope that it would give southern voters more of a say in the nomination process. In recent elections, however, Super Tuesday has produced mixed results. In 1988, Super Tuesday provided a surge of voting in the Republican ranks, as supporters of George Bush turned out in big numbers. The Democratic vote was split among several candidates.

The early caucus and primary contests are the first step in seeking the presidential nomination. They can earn a candidate approval and recognition. But the primaries that follow can be just as important to a candidate.

George Bush used the Iowa caucuses in 1980 to help him emerge from obscurity. Although Bush had held a number of key government posts—he served as head of the CIA and was the United States' delegate to the United Nations—he was not very well known to voters. His victory in Iowa changed that. Bush, however, was ultimately defeated by Ronald Reagan in his bid for the Republican nomination that year.

In 1976, Democrat Jimmy Carter, then fifty-two years old, a former peanut farmer, naval officer, and one-term governor of Georgia, gave a clear-cut demonstration of how to use the primaries to win the nomination. At the time, hardly anyone knew who Carter was. Nobody "important" supported him. He was, in fact, so little known that when he entered the race late in 1974 and announced who he was, people asked, "Jimmy who?" Even his mother couldn't understand what he was trying to do. When he told her he was running for President, she asked, "President of what?"

As Carter traveled about the country meeting people, he offered a simple message. He said he would never indulge in the kind of secrecy that produced the Vietnam War and the Watergate scandal.

George Bush holds up a victory T-shirt following his win in the Super Tuesday primaries in 1988.

"I will never lie," he proclaimed. "I will never make misleading statements."

While Carter got only 29 percent of the vote in the Iowa caucus, no one candidate got any more than that, and he was hailed as the big winner. After he led the field in the New Hampshire primary, Carter's face began appearing on the covers of *Time* and *Newsweek*. Almost overnight, he had become the candidate to beat.

Carter went on to win primaries in Florida, Illinois, and North Carolina. In April, he captured the Pennsylvania and Washington primaries. Jimmy Carter won more than half of the thirty primaries he entered.

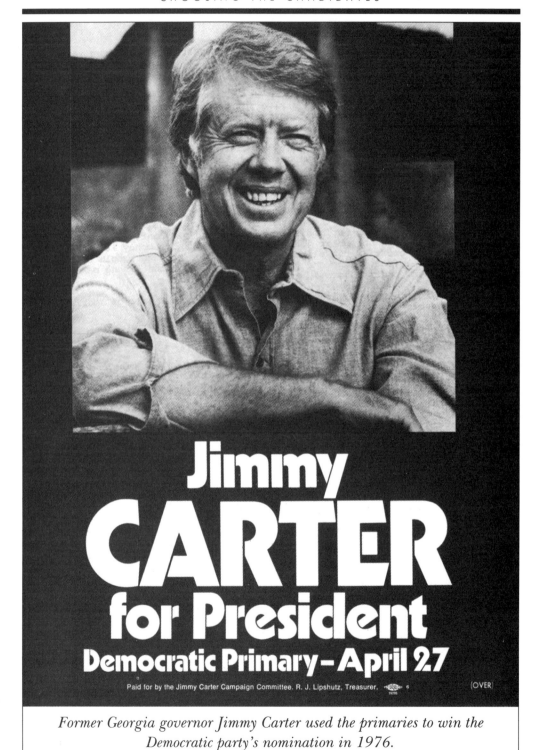

Jimmy
CARTER
for President
Democratic Primary – April 27

Paid for by the Jimmy Carter Campaign Committee. R. J. Lipshutz, Treasurer. 6

(OVER)

Former Georgia governor Jimmy Carter used the primaries to win the Democratic party's nomination in 1976.

Jimmy Carter gives a victory wave at the 1976 Democratic convention.

The fact that the Democrats had abolished unit rule, that is, winner-take-all primaries, four years before was a big help to Carter. He received delegates in direct proportion to the number of votes he got. So although he was defeated in five of the last eight primaries which he entered, Carter kept right on accumulating delegates. At the Democratic convention that summer, the delegates picked Jimmy Carter on the first ballot. That fall the voters gave him a narrow victory over Gerald Ford, who had advanced to the White House after Richard Nixon's resignation in 1974.

While primaries can lead to the big prize, they also can have a deadly effect, serving to eliminate a candidate from the race. After Senator Edward Kennedy lost to President Jimmy Carter in the Illinois primary in 1979 by a 2 to 1 margin in the popular vote and 165 to 14 in delegates, it was taken to mean that Kennedy could not win a heavily populated, ethnic, industrial state. From then on, Kennedy's campaign was doomed.

More recently, in 1988, the campaign of Robert Dole, George Bush's chief rival, fell apart on Super Tuesday. His staff members quarreled and he ran out of campaign funds. As Bush vaulted far into the lead, Dole had no choice but to quit the race.

Criticisms of Primaries and Caucuses

Suggestions for changing the primary election process are heard frequently. Many voters believe that Iowa and New Hampshire have too great an influence on who ultimately gets nominated. By the time voters in other states go to the polls, Iowa and New Hampshire may have pretty much decided matters, critics say. A filtering process has narrowed the choices as a result.

Some experts have suggested that a more orderly system be put into effect. They want the states to spread out the primaries and caucuses, with voting only on the first Tuesday in March, April, May, and June. Still, in almost any system, one state will always come first. It's a privilege that cannot be denied.

Senator Paul Simon of Illinois, a candidate for the Democratic nomination in 1988, found no fault with the Iowa caucuses and New Hampshire primary. He praised them, in fact. He felt that Iowa and New Hampshire gave candidates with a limited amount of money a chance for the nomination that they might not have gotten otherwise. "People in Iowa and New Hampshire do not give their commitments lightly," Senator Simon declared in an article in the *New York Times*. "No one through money alone can walk away with either state."

Some political observers say there is nothing wrong with the primaries. Rather, it is the caucuses that cause problems. These observers point to the low voter turnout in caucuses—usually around 10 percent of the party's registered voters. The state of Iowa, where there has been greater voter participation, is an exception, however.

There are other criticisms of caucuses. They produce unequal results because they reward the candidates who appeal to political activists. For example, the big winners in the caucuses in 1988 were television evangelist Pat Robertson and Jesse Jackson. Both candidates had highly enthusiastic supporters. When Jesse Jackson received 115,000 votes in Michigan, his victory was treated almost the same as a victory in a state where millions voted.

The ordinary voter is known to make responsible choices. But in the caucuses, ordinary voters are overwhelmed by activists. It has been suggested that states with caucuses switch to primaries.

One other often heard suggestion is to replace the present system with a national primary, a day set aside when all fifty states would offer primary elections. But this proposal has never made much headway. Only established candidates would have enough money to finance a national primary campaign. Candidates lacking in funds would never enter the race. In other words, a national primary would tend to favor the front-runners; new faces would be at a disadvantage.

Much the same criticism has been aimed at regional primaries such as Super Tuesday. They favor candidates who have the organization and money to campaign in twenty or more states simultaneously. Underdogs get buried on Super Tuesday. They can usually only campaign in one state at a time.

Sifting the Candidates in 1988

The present system of primaries and caucuses has been applauded because it serves as a sifting process. By its length and difficulty, it exposes those who lack character or tend toward mismanagement. At the same time, it usually rewards candidates who have qualities voters seek.

Consider what happened in 1988, the year the nominating process produced Democrat Michael Dukakis and Republican George Bush as candidates. The Democrats sifted through seven presidential hopefuls in 1987. The men who planned to campaign for their party's nomination were an intelligent and experienced group, but they were not very well known, and no one individual stood out. The media responded by nicknaming the Democratic contenders the Seven Dwarfs.

| Bush | Dole | Robertson | Kemp | Gore |

| Jackson | Gephardt | Simon | Hart | Dukakis |

Some of the presidential candidates in 1988. The final candidates were George Bush and Michael Dukakis.

The five Republican candidates escaped being branded with such a nickname. Yet they, like the Democrats, said very little that inspired or excited anyone, at least in the early stages of the campaign. None of the candidates "utters a word that lifts your heart," said a leading Illinois Democrat.

The problem may have been not with the candidates but with the times. In 1987, there was no one great issue to electrify voters. Americans know how to use the ballot box to express their feelings. In 1968, when the war in Vietnam was raging, voters boosted antiwar candidates Eugene McCarthy and Robert Kennedy toward the presidency and shoved President Lyndon Johnson out of the race. When Iranians seized the United States Embassy in Iran in 1979 and held fifty-two Americans hostage, the nation was shocked and angry. When President Jimmy Carter was unable to free the

*Michael Dukakis campaigns for the presidency in Jersey City,
New Jersey, in 1988.*

hostages, the voters turned him out of office in favor of Ronald Reagan. But in 1987, the voters were generally content.

Actually, the twelve Democrats and Republicans in 1987 offered the American voters a wide choice of able and experienced candidates. Of the twelve, all but one had graduated from college. And the one exception (Senator Paul Simon of Illinois) had a record of thirty years in elective service and was the author of several books and a weekly newspaper column. Several of the candidates had graduated with honors.

One of the candidates had been a two-term Vice-President; three had been governors; four, senators; eight, members of the House of Representatives.

Five of the candidates had been successful in business. There were six lawyers, three authors, and a former professional quarterback. Two had been chairmen of their national political parties.

Several of the candidates had served on presidential commissions. One had been supreme allied commander, White House chief of staff, and secretary of state. Another had been a vice-presidential candidate and both majority and minority leader of the Senate. The candidates had seen service in the National Guard, the army, the marines, and the navy.

When Democrat Michael Dukakis, governor of Massachusetts, and Republican George Bush, then in his eighth year as Ronald Reagan's Vice-President, emerged from the long struggle as their party's nominees, no one should have been surprised. They were both steady and dependable. They had been fair and honorable as public servants. They managed their campaigns carefully, cautiously, step by step. They had all the qualities many Americans found attractive in 1988 when it came to choosing a President. In that sense, the system worked.

CHAPTER EIGHT

WHY A CONVENTION?

The primaries and caucuses over, the remaining candidates make their way to the presidential nominating conventions. These conventions have been part of the political scene since the early 1830s. Since that time, few have equaled the Democratic convention of 1924 for suspense. It was held at Madison Square Garden in New York City in the midst of a steamy heat wave.

On June 24, opening day, the leading candidates for the nomination were Alfred E. Smith, the popular governor of New York, and California's William McAdoo, who had served as secretary of state during the administration of Woodrow Wilson. Once the voting got underway, the delegates were unable to choose between the two men. One ballot followed another without a decision being reached. At the time, the rules required a two-thirds majority to nominate. This rule stayed in effect until 1936.

Day after day passed and the convention remained deadlocked. A week went by. Fourth of July loomed. Humorist Will

Rogers noted that New York City had invited the delegates to visit the place, not to live there.

Not only were there a record number of ballots cast, but more speeches were heard, more committee meetings held, and more demonstrations staged than at any other convention in history.

On the convention's ninth day, Smith and McAdoo withdrew their names, releasing their exhausted delegates to vote as they pleased. More ballots were taken. By now, the convention was into its second week.

Finally, on the seventeenth day, after the 103d ballot, the nomination went to John W. Davis, a New York lawyer from West Virginia who had served as President Wilson's ambassador to Great Britain. Although Davis worked hard during the campaign, he was soundly defeated by Republican Calvin Coolidge.

Four years earlier, it had taken the Democrats 44 ballots to nominate James M. Cox, who lost to Warren G. Harding in the election of 1920.

Nominations that take 44 or 103 ballots have gone the way of free road maps and doctors' house calls.

Nowadays, the names of those who are to be the Democratic and Republican nominees are known months before the delegates leave home for the convention site. The lack of suspense in today's convention nominating process is due to a change in the role of delegates. Convention delegates are no longer controlled by their delegation leaders. They are in most cases pledged to follow the will of the voters in their state's primary or caucus.

A Symbol of Politics

If the outcome of the nominating convention is known, then why not do the balloting by mail? Why bother to have a convention at all?

National conventions still play a vital role in the American political process. In fact, they are *the* symbol of politics in the United States.

Despite the fact that the name of the nominee is known, the results must be confirmed by a majority of the convention delegates. In other words, the convention makes the choice official.

The convention also serves as a backstop. Representative Barney Frank of Massachusetts has called it "the nominator of last resort." Says Frank: "It's there to enable us to pick someone if the caucuses and primaries fail to do so."

Conventions also help to make the presidential nominating process truly national. Under the existing system, the party organizations in the fifty states function almost as independent units. Then one week every four years, those fifty state organizations assemble to write a party platform, adopt party rules, and nominate a presidential candidate.

In the process, various factions within the party get to express their opinions. There may be a real tug of war between those representing conflicting points of view. The drama may be acted out in full view of the media. This is healthy for the party and important to the voters.

The convention is also a unifying force for the party. Throughout 1988, Paul G. Kirk, Jr., the chairperson of the Democratic party, insisted that the party must rally behind the candidate with the most delegate support when the convention started, even if that candidate happened to be well short of a majority. And during the convention itself, after Massachusetts Governor Michael Dukakis had gotten the endorsement of the delegates, he also won the backing of the party's left, right, and center. On top of that, he earned the promise of support from Jesse Jackson, his most successful rival. Significantly, on the night the roll call of the states was taken, Jackson stayed in his hotel suite with his family and a few aides. He did so because he did not want to steal attention from Dukakis in his moment of triumph.

More and more, the nominating convention has come to be viewed as a launching pad for the campaign. It serves as a stage where the party can present its new candidate before a worldwide television audience. When Michael Dukakis delivered his acceptance speech at the Democratic National Convention in 1988, he stressed the two historic ideals of the Democratic party: economic well-being and spirited public service. The delegates greeted his words with prolonged cheers and thunderous applause. No one doubted it was the official opening of Dukakis's drive for the White House.

When and Where to Hold the Convention?

Long before the convention opens, party committees are at work. They must find a city in which to hold the convention, arrange for a meeting site within that city, and assure housing, credentials, and badges for the delegates and their alternates. Party committees must also provide facilities for the media. This in itself is a big chore. At the Democratic convention in Atlanta in 1988, credentials were issued to more than 12,500 members of the press, radio, and television.

Political parties take great care in deciding when and where to hold their conventions. A date between mid-July and late August is usually chosen. The "out" party—the party not in possession of the presidency at the time—normally holds its convention before the "in" party. In 1988, when Republican Ronald Reagan occupied the White House, the Democrats scheduled their convention several weeks before the Republicans so they could take advantage of the added time to campaign provided by their earlier convention.

Cities profit when chosen as convention sites. A week-long visit of many thousands of delegates, their families and friends, plus the exposure provided by national television, means many millions of dollars to a city's economy.

At one time, parties encouraged cities to make sizable financial contributions as a qualification for being picked as a convention site. The money came not only from the city administration but from the city's hotels and restaurants, which stood to benefit the most from the influx of visitors. But in the wake of the Watergate scandal of the early 1970s, the practice was halted. Nowadays, each of the two major parties receives $8 million from the federal government to finance its nominating convention.

With cash no longer so important in selecting a convention site, other factors are weighed more carefully. These include the size and

ABC television's broadcast booth looms above the state delegations at the 1988 Democratic convention in Atlanta.

The 1964 Democratic convention in Atlantic City, New Jersey, which nominated Lyndon B. Johnson.

facilities of the convention arena, the size and efficiency of the local police force, and the number and quality of the city's hotel and motel rooms. The importance of housing should never be underestimated. In 1968, when Chicago and Philadelphia were both being considered as sites for the Democratic convention, the nod went to Chicago because Philadelphia was then unable to provide 20,000 first-class rooms required by the conventioneers.

Other factors can also be important in choosing a convention site. Security is a major concern for the candidates and delegates. Street riots were a sad feature of the 1968 Democratic National Convention. When the Democrats picked Miami Beach four years later, they did so partly because of the existence of a causeway over Biscayne Bay leading to the convention hall. Miami police were thus able to isolate the convention site from potential demonstrators.

When the Republicans selected Miami Beach in 1968, it marked the first time the party ever held its convention in the South. The move was taken to indicate the Republicans were beginning to regard the southern states and their voters in a much more serious manner. In 1988, both parties went south. The Democrats picked Atlanta; the Republicans, New Orleans.

Opening Day

On the opening day of the convention, the delegates assemble, with each state delegation seated together. Each party has its own way of alloting votes to the state delegations and can change that allotment from one convention to the next. In 1988, the Democrats had 4,163 delegates while the Republicans had 2,277.

The chairperson of the party's national committee delivers a welcoming address, praising the record of his or her party and lashing out at the opposition. Four committees are selected through roll calls of the states: the Committee on Credentials, the Committee on Permanent Organization, the Committee on Rules and Order of Business, and the Committee on Platform and Resolutions. Each state is entitled to one member on each of these four committees.

The Committee on Credentials plays an all-important role during the convention. It has the responsibility of settling the rival claims of persons claiming membership in the convention. Usually there are only a few disputes and these are resolved peacefully. But occasionally there are many seats in dispute, and a heated debate can result.

During the Republican National Convention in Chicago in 1952, a contest between Dwight D. Eisenhower, the World War II hero, and Senator Robert Taft of Ohio, featured a bitter dispute over sixty-eight delegate seats of Texas, Georgia, and Louisiana. Taft's loss of the three delegations forecast Eisenhower's victory.

When the Democrats met in Atlantic City in 1964, trouble erupted over the seating of delegates from Mississippi. The regular delegation, all whites, was challenged by the mainly black "Mississippi Freedom Democratic party." A compromise was hammered out that gave the Freedom Democrats two convention seats. More important, the agreement established an antidiscrimination requirement for all Democratic party groups assigned to name delegates to future conventions. Although the compromise was rejected, its anti-discrimination theme heralded important changes that were to be made in the selection of delegates in 1968, 1972, and even to this day.

After the matter of credentials has been settled and the roll of delegates has been officially established, the Committee on Permanent Organization brings in its reports, nominating a permanent chairperson and other convention officials. After the nominations are accepted, the newly elected chairperson delivers the keynote address, presenting the party's principles and policies and its stance on important issues of the day. Other leading personalities of the party also address the convention.

An address can showcase a political figure. When New York Governor Mario Cuomo spoke before the Democratic National Convention in 1984, he stressed the themes of compassion and social equality. When he urged the party to unite behind Walter Mondale and Geraldine Ferraro, he stirred a swell of emotional applause and cheers. The next day, people began talking about Cuomo as a presidential candidate of the future.

As the convention gets underway, other committees meet and issue reports. The Committee on Rules and Order of Business usually adopts the rules of the previous convention. But sometimes this committee can issue a rule that turns things upside down. At the Democratic convention in 1936, for example, the committee abolished the two-thirds rule. This made it possible for a candidate to be nominated by a simple majority rather than by two-thirds of the vote.

The Committee on Platform and Resolutions is usually the last to report. The platform is a statement of the party's stands on major issues of the day. In 1988, party platforms were concerned with such issues as the arms race, the drug problem, jobs, and help for the poor.

8:20	Chairman Wright reconvenes the convention and recognizes former Vice President Walter M. Mondale and Joan Mondale.
8:25	Videotape: "WE THE DELEGATES".
8:28	Chairman Wright recognizes Bruce Babbitt, former Governor of Arizona, and former candidate for president.
8:30	Chairman Wright pays tribute to American cities and introduces George Latimer, Mayor of St. Paul, Minnesota.
8:33	Mayor Latimer introduces Andrew Young, Mayor of Atlanta, Georgia.
8:35	Mayor Andrew Young welcomes the convention to Atlanta.
8:42	Chairman Wright introduces Barbara Boxer, U.S. Congresswoman, State of California.
8:43	Congresswoman Boxer addresses the convention and introduces Booth Gardner, Governor, State of Washington.
8:46	Governor Gardner speaks on "The Democratic Party's Task: Solving Problems of Real People for the 1990s".

Convention activities are planned on a minute-by-minute basis as shown by the schedule for the 1988 Democratic convention.

There are two different approaches to writing a platform. In the case of the party in power, the platform is usually written under the scrutiny of presidential advisers, then submitted to the convention for approval. There is seldom much criticism of the platform in this case, so long as the President is popular with the party.

In the case of the party not in power, the National Committee supervises the writing of the platform, forming a committee that represents special-interest groups and the leading candidates.

Sometimes there are heated arguments over platform planks. Committee members have the difficult task of trying to satisfy conflicting points of view while producing a platform with real meaning.

A debate over the platform was one of the features of the Democratic National Convention of 1980. As far as the voting was concerned, it was obvious from the opening session that President Jimmy Carter would defeat his challenger, Senator Edward Kennedy. But stubborn Kennedy supporters, eager to steal the show, battled Carter over platform planks and got the President to modify his stand on several issues. The dispute carried over until the very end of the convention. On the final evening, when the party leaders assembled on the podium, Kennedy was late in arriving and then refused to raise his hands with Carter in a show of unity.

The Role of Television

The discord within the Democratic ranks in 1980 was obvious to the millions who watched on television that night. For hours afterward, television newscasters discussed and analyzed what had just been shown. Clearly, television plays a dominant role in national conventions. Ever since 1952, when television began to cover the conventions, the medium's importance has grown and grown. Today, coverage is provided by the three major television networks — CBS, NBC, ABC — and a variety of cable news and public affairs channels. Television newscasters from local stations also manage to wedge their way onto the convention floor.

But while the number of networks and local stations providing coverage has expanded, the number of television viewers has been declining. During the 1988 conventions, television ratings showed a substantial drop in viewership compared to 1984.

On any given night of convention coverage in 1988, the individual ratings of each of the major networks was far below the level attained by such then top-ranked programs as "The Cosby Show." Convention coverage was below the ratings achieved by standard entertainment and, on some independent stations, below the ratings of old movies.

One reason why fewer people watched the conventions in 1988 was lack of excitement and drama. In past conventions, delegates debated issues and selected candidates. Conventions were, as television network executives pointed out, a kind of civics lesson given every four years.

National television coverage of a convention started in 1952. Dwight D. Eisenhower was the Republican nominee that year.

At recent conventions, as the suspense factor has lessened and ratings have dropped, the attitude of the television networks has changed. In 1968, for instance, the three major networks presented as much as fifty hours of live coverage during convention week. In 1988, for the Democratic convention in Atlanta and the Republican convention in New Orleans, the networks reduced coverage to less than fifteen hours.

*A shower of confetti greets George Bush (center), Dan Quayle (right),
and their families at the 1988 Republican convention.*

At one time, the networks telecast convention events as they unfolded. By the 1980s, the networks had become more selective. Sometimes, the networks resisted attempts to turn coverage into pure propaganda. In 1984, for example, when the Republicans wanted to show a film in praise of Ronald Reagan, two of the networks — CBS and NBC — refused to put it on the air. In 1988, a biographical film about Jimmy Carter was ignored by all three networks. One of the networks, CBS, decided not to show a filmed profile of Jesse Jackson that was to run just before a Jackson speech. "It was a straight-out political film," said CBS anchorperson Dan Rather. "If they want this kind of stuff on TV, they should buy time."

At the Republican convention in New Orleans in 1988, leaders of George Bush's campaign fully understood the importance of television coverage. In their view, speeches inside the Louisiana Superdome would be of little importance to voters unless their candidate's message was sent out to the millions of television viewers. Consequently, Bush's people spent months planning a convention program that would appeal to the television networks and their viewers. "A convention made for TV," the *New York Times* called it.

The Republicans picked a different theme for each day. On Monday, the convention's opening day, the theme was the success of the Reagan-Bush administration. The highlight of that night's telecast was a dramatic speech by President Reagan.

Tuesday was called "comparison day." A series of speakers stressed George Bush's strengths and reviewed what they felt to be Michael Dukakis's weaknesses. (Dukakis had been picked as the Democratic candidate several weeks before.)

On Wednesday, when the roll-call vote of the states was taken and the candidate received his party's official endorsement, Bush's qualifications for office were emphasized. It was also a night of flag-waving and political speech-making.

On Thursday, Bush's acceptance speech was scheduled. It was to be a night of triumph and celebration. But the program did not follow the script. It was marred by the controversy over Bush's surprise choice of Dan Quayle as his running mate.

For each day of the convention, the speakers were chosen with the greatest of care. Fred V. Malek, the convention manager, alloted carefully measured amounts of time to each of several different types of speakers. According to Malek, 11 percent of the time the speaker would be an American of Hispanic descent, 12 percent of the time a black, and 40 percent of the time a woman.

Bush campaign officials also tried to exert control over what each person had to say. Speakers had to submit their remarks in advance for review by campaign officials.

Not every speaker could be controlled. Alan L. Keyes, the Republican candidate for the Senate in Maryland, objected when he was asked to talk about how proud he was to be both a black and Republican. Keyes threatened not to speak at all unless he was given the right to talk about a subject of his own choosing. Bush's supporters backed down.

The Democrats also planned their 1988 convention with one eye on television. The production team hired to decorate Atlanta's Omni Coliseum for the convention decided that the colors red, white, and blue looked "cheap" on television. They replaced them with shades of salmon, eggshell, and azure for a brighter, fresher look. The podium on which Dukakis made his acceptance speech was equipped with a hydraulic lift that made the five-foot-eight-inch Dukakis and Lloyd Bentsen, his six-foot-two-inch running mate, appear to be the same height.

When television first began to cover presidential nominating conventions, some people were fearful. They believed television would influence voters to choose candidates for their good looks and little else. That hasn't happened yet. But we keep getting closer.

CHAPTER NINE

PARTICIPANTS AND PREJUDICES

Once the convention has gotten underway and party rules have been established, party leaders have been chosen, and the platform has been debated, written, and adopted, the delegates prepare for their main task—nominating the party's candidates for President and Vice-President. At the nominating session, the chairperson calls on each state in alphabetical order for nominations. The spokesperson for a delegation may place a name in nomination or yield to a state that wishes to nominate a candidate.

Each nominating speech praises the candidate in lavish terms and builds to a final, climactic announcement of the person's name. That touches off an uproar. Balloons are released, the band plays loudly, and placard-carrying supporters of the candidate sing and cheer.

At one time, these outbursts were meant to win over delegates who might be wavering in their support of one candidate or another. But today, with almost all of the delegates already committed, floor demonstrations are conducted more for the benefit of television cameras than anything else. They are a colorful relic of the past.

After a demonstration has ended, seconding speeches are heard. These, too, trigger demonstrations, but they are not quite as lengthy as those that follow the initial announcement.

When all of the nominations have been entered, the roll call of the states, again in alphabetical order, begins. A delegation spokesperson announces the number of votes cast for each candidate.

In conventions of the past, delegate voting was exciting and suspenseful. Would the leading candidate compile enough votes to win? Or would some dark horse suddenly show strength, diminishing the chances of the favorite? In some conventions, no one really knew what to expect from one ballot to the next. Nowadays there is more suspense in watching grass grow. The call of the roll merely gives each state delegation a few minutes to shine for the hometown folks. It's show business. As soon as one candidate has polled a majority of the delegates, that person is declared the party's nominee.

Interestingly, in the case of both the Democrats and Republicans, the long screening process invariably produces candidates with a certain sameness. They are usually white, Anglo-Saxon, Protestant males. Being a woman, non-Christian, black, Hispanic, Native American, or Asian is a handicap in seeking to represent one of the major parties as a presidential nominee.

The Role of Gender and Race

Patricia (Pat) Schroeder, from Denver, Colorado, with fifteen years experience as a member of Congress, made a brief run for the 1988 presidential nomination. She did it because she believed, as she put it, "America is man enough to back a woman."

Schroeder began her campaign in mid-1987 but quit the race early in the fall, before any caucuses or primary elections had taken place. An important reason she decided to drop out had to do with money, or lack of it. She had raised about a million dollars, which,

SENATOR
Margaret Chase
SMITH
for PRESIDENT

 VOTE REPUBLICAN

Maine Senator Margaret Chase Smith was the first woman to seek the presidency for a major party.

she judged, was about half the amount she needed. "I refused to conduct a campaign in the red," she said. "How could I go around the country speaking out against the national debt if I was running up a debt myself?"

Schroeder also felt she had no "top-notch staff." Her decision to run had been made almost on the spur of the moment, so she lacked the kind of campaign organization that other candidates spent years planning and assembling.

Another of Schroeder's concerns was the tendency of the press to look upon her as a "woman's candidate for President."

Americans are making progress toward accepting the idea of a woman President, Schroeder said in her book, *Champion of the Great American Family.* Nevertheless, she added, women still don't "look presidential" to many voters. "At least, I didn't," she said. "My laugh, my signature, my mannerisms, were seen as too feminine. I was told that in politics boyish charm is fine but girlish charm is out of place."

If Schroeder had pursued the campaign, she would have been the first woman to run for President since Representative Shirley Chisholm of Brooklyn, New York, the first black woman to serve in the United States Congress, had sought the nomination in 1972. Mar-

Reverend Jesse Jackson (left) shares a light moment with New York Congressman Charles Rangel. Jackson sought the Democratic presidential nomination in 1984 and 1988.

garet Chase Smith, a United States senator from Maine, campaigned for the Republican presidential nomination in 1964, the first woman to ever do so for a major party.

A survey conducted by the *Washington Post* and ABC News showed that many voters are not enthusiastic about candidates who are female. According to the poll, taken in mid-1987 and based on telephone interviews with 1,506 adults, slightly more than one-fourth of Americans said they would be less likely to vote for a presidential candidate who is a woman.

Voters have also shown some reluctance to cast their ballots for a presidential candidate who is black. In 1983, civil rights leader Jesse Jackson challenged the Democratic party to nominate a black for President in 1984, and then announced his own candidacy. Although his campaign was late getting started and he ran on a shoestring budget, Jesse Jackson won 19 percent of the Democratic primary votes and 11 percent of the delegates, which enabled him to finish third behind Walter F. Mondale and Colorado Senator Gary Hart.

Jackson made another try in 1988. He was much better organized and raised about a million dollars, enough to mount a campaign, he said, although it was a good deal less than most of his opponents.

In polls taken early in the campaign, Jackson had more support than any other Democrat seeking the presidential nomination. A poll taken by the *New York Times* and CBS News early in 1987 showed that Jackson ranked number one ahead of Governor Michael Dukakis of Massachusetts, Senator Paul Simon of Illinois, and five other candidates.

But there were whispers that Jackson could never win the nomination. The reason? Race.

"Race is a severe limit on Jackson," Ron Walters, professor of political science at Howard University and an adviser to Jackson, told the *Washington Post*. "When people say to me, 'What is a black guy doing running for President?' and beneath that is the question, 'Should a black man be President — do I want to be represented by a black President?' This is very deep. People will not come out and say it, but that is the case."

The voting pattern during the 1988 primaries confirmed that race was a big factor. Take Illinois, for instance. Jackson was a Chicagoan and Illinois had been his political base for two decades. But in the voting in the Illinois primary, Jackson managed to get only 7 percent of the white vote, according to a *New York Times*-CBS poll of voters. Jackson took, as expected, 90 percent of the black vote. But it wasn't enough to win or even come close. Senator Paul Simon of Illinois swept the contests for convention delegates, beating Jackson on a better than three-to-one basis.

Linda Williams, an election specialist at the Joint Center for Political Studies, a black-oriented research organization in Washington, said it was possible for Jackson to win the nomination. "But it isn't at all likely," she told the *New York Times*. "Without a stronger showing among whites, he won't end up as the leader in delegates, and even if he does, I think the party leaders — the super delegates, governors, senators—will join together to stop him." (Ms. Williams was right; the convention's super delegates voted in a bloc against Jackson.)

One Democratic official outlined the hopelessness of Jackson's cause. "Let's look at November," he said. "Give him 100 percent of the black vote and 20 percent of the white vote, twice what he's been getting. He doesn't come close to carrying a big state."

While some polls showed Jackson to have voter strength, the party professionals as a whole did not believe the figures, said the *New York Times.* "They remain convinced," the newspaper declared, "that no black nominee, and especially one with policy stands like Mr. Jackson's, can be elected President; indeed, they doubt that a ticket including Mr. Jackson as vice-presidential nominee would stand any significant chance."

Once Michael Dukakis had nailed down the Democratic nomination, Jackson hinted he might be interested in being nominated Vice-President. Polls then showed that he would do more harm than good as Dukakis's running mate. Said Benjamin L. Hooks, executive director of the National Association for the Advancement of Colored People (NAACP): "I would advise Jackson not to take the vice-presidency, even if it is offered, because you have to understand that I do not believe that this nation is prepared to elect a black as Vice-President."

Some voters spurned Jackson for reasons other than those having to do with race. His positions on more than a few issues, particularly foreign policy issues, were outside the mainstream of Democratic politics. For example, the one issue on which Jackson directly criticized his opponents concerned South Africa and its official policy of racial segregation, apartheid. "They must take a stand to end apartheid, not just be against it," Jackson said of his rivals. In addition, Jackson was the only presidential candidate in 1988 who wanted to require all American companies to leave South Africa by a specific date.

On the national scene, Jesse Jackson proposed deep cuts in U.S. military spending. At the same time, he called for increased spending on day-care, public and preschool education, Social Security, welfare payments, housing for low-income families, and job training.

Jackson's lack of political experience was another reason that some voters turned their backs on him. He had never held elective office.

What Kind of Candidate?

Presidential candidates almost always have had experience in the national government, state government, or both. It is a fact that, since 1900, all of the nation's Presidents, except Dwight D. Eisenhower, a World War II general, have come from the ranks of senators, congressional representatives, governors, or cabinet members. Fourteen Vice-Presidents and fifteen governors have become President.

In earlier times, military leaders were sought as presidential candidates. Andrew Jackson, Zachary Taylor, Ulysses S. Grant, and, as mentioned, Dwight D. Eisenhower were noted battlefield generals before being elected President. William Henry Harrison first won fame as an Indian fighter.

George Washington, of course, was a military hero, but his principal occupation was that of plantation owner.

Even today, military service of one type or another is almost always considered a political asset. George Bush was a naval aviator during World War II. Ronald Reagan served in the United States Army Air Corps. Twenty-six of the forty Presidents saw military service.

Whether emerging from the ranks of the military or elsewhere, presidential candidates are expected to have led near-perfect lives in moral and ethical terms. A candidate's conduct must be able to withstand the closest scrutiny. At one time, a divorce could weigh heavily against someone with the ambition to be President. It did not, however, prevent Adlai Stevenson from becoming the Democratic nominee in 1952 and again in 1956; nor was it any great obstacle to Ronald Reagan, who was twice elected President.

While divorce is no longer considered to be particularly damaging to the ambitions of a candidate, the hint of scandal is very

Dwight D. Eisenhower was one of the nation's many military leaders elected President.

harmful. There is, for example, the case of Senator Edward Kennedy of Massachusetts, who ranked as the leading candidate for the 1972 Democratic nomination. Then, one July night in 1969, Kennedy's automobile plunged off a bridge in Chappaquiddick, Massachusetts. A young woman riding with Senator Kennedy in the car was killed. That, plus his evasive behavior in the days that followed, earned Kennedy heated criticism. In January 1971, he dropped out of the race.

In 1980, Edward Kennedy decided to try again, challenging President Jimmy Carter for the Democratic nomination. When he entered the race on Labor Day 1979, the polls showed Kennedy to be leading Carter in popularity. Perhaps Kennedy thought Chappaquiddick had been forgotten.

Kennedy campaigned vigorously in Iowa, the first state to hold elections for delegates to the Democratic National Convention. Chappaquiddick became an issue. Carter's television ads in Iowa hinted that Kennedy had not told the whole truth about the tragedy. When they went to the polls, Iowa voters picked twice as many delegates for Carter as for Kennedy.

The New Hampshire primary followed close on the heels of the voting in Iowa. There, Kennedy sought to appeal to Americans' sense of fair play. In a televised speech, he said, "While I know many will never believe the facts of the tragic events at Chappaquiddick, those facts are the only truth I can tell because that is the way it happened, and I ask only to be judged on the basic American standards of fairness." The strategy failed; again Kennedy finished second to Carter.

As the primary season continued, Kennedy began gaining in popularity. In fact, the Massachusetts senator won five of the last eight primaries. Nevertheless, Carter accumulated more than enough delegates to ensure his nomination on the first ballot. Chappaquiddick was too great a scandal for Senator Edward Kennedy to overcome.

Gary Hart of Colorado, who made an attempt to capture the Democratic nomination in 1988, is a more recent example of how scandal can harm a political career. Earlier, when Hart had run for the Senate in 1974 and made a try for the Democratic nomination in 1984, he admitted to having marital problems. Twice he and his wife had separated. There were questions about his having dated several other women while still married to his wife.

In 1987, Hart made another try for the nomination. For a time, he ranked as the Democrats' front-runner. Then the press began to focus on his personal life and character. A newspaper reported that Hart had spent a weekend at his Washington town house and time on a yacht with a model. As a result of the story, Hart was soon engulfed in a storm of controversy. He tried to blame the press. The tactic did not work. The scandal would not go away and Gary Hart withdrew from the race.

Later in the year, Hart, in a surprise move, resumed his campaign for the nomination. Few people took him seriously, however, and he dropped out a second time.

At one time, religion was an important consideration in choosing presidential candidates. Except for John F. Kennedy, American

VOTE APRIL 22

SEE and HEAR

Senator

EDWARD KENNEDY

Monday, April 21
12:00 Noon

Corner of
15th & Chestnut Streets
Center City   Philadelphia

PULL LEVER #104

Volunteers Welcome
Call 732-0794
or come to
216 South 16th St.
Philadelphia

Paid for by Kennedy for President Committee, Carolyn Reed, Treas. A copy of our report is filed with and available for purchase from the F.E.C. Washington, D.C.

Personal problems hurt Edward Kennedy in his bid for the presidency.

New York State Governor Alfred E. Smith, the Democratic candidate,
lost to Herbert Hoover in the election of 1928.

Presidents have been Protestants. The election of 1928 in which Democrat Alfred E. Smith, a Catholic, faced Republican Herbert Hoover, brought the subject of religion into a sharp focus.

Born in 1873, Alfred E. Smith grew up on the sidewalks of New York City. He worked as an errand boy and a clerk and went into politics as a young man. Down-to-earth, wisecracking, and popular, Smith served as a legislator in the New York State Assembly and was a governor for four terms. His friend Franklin D. Roosevelt nominated Smith for President at the 1928 Democratic convention, calling him the "Happy Warrior." Smith was chosen on the first ballot.

Smith's Republican opponent, Herbert Hoover, was a mining engineer who had risen to the post of secretary of commerce. Bland and humorless, Hoover's personality was in sharp contrast to the easygoing Smith.

Religion did not decide the election of 1928 but it was an important factor. Even before he became a presidential candidate, Smith had made it clear that he believed in "the absolute separation" of church and state in America. "I have taken the oath of office nineteen times," he said. "Each time I swore to defend and maintain the Constitution of the United States."

But there were wild rumors about Smith's being Catholic. It was said that the pope was ready to move to Washington as soon as Smith had won the election; he had his bags already packed. It was said that Smith was planning to extend New York City's newly opened Holland Tunnel under the Atlantic Ocean to the basement of the pope's headquarters in Vatican City. Anti-Catholic literature was distributed in enormous quantities throughout the country. When Smith went to Oklahoma City to make a campaign speech, his route to the auditorium was lined with burning crosses placed by the Ku Klux Klan.

Smith's advisers wanted him to ignore the anti-Catholic attacks rather than call attention to them. But Smith was so angered at some of the things that were being said and done, he could not help but speak out.

Another important issue in the election of 1928 was prohibition, the legal banning of the sale of alcoholic beverages. Prohibition had become the law of the land in 1919 with the ratification of the Eighteenth Amendment. Hoover believed the Eighteenth Amendment should be strictly enforced. Smith was a "wet," that is, he favored allowing states the right to pass laws permitting the sale of beer and wine, if they desired.

Being from New York City did not help Smith, either. He represented big-city politics. A political machine and political bosses had helped to get him where he was.

All of these things — being a Catholic, a "wet," and representing the New York political machine — hurt Smith in rural America. During the campaign, huge, enthusiastic crowds turned out to hear Smith in big cities. In the South and West, however, people rejected him.

Hoover scored a lopsided victory, carrying 58 percent of the popular vote and 40 (of the then 48) states. Smith believed that his religion cost him the election. There was no doubt that he lost some votes because he was Catholic, but he was also hurt by his stand on prohibition and his association with New York politics.

When Postmaster General James Farley, a Catholic, made a try for the presidency in 1940, he also felt the sting of prejudice. According to Robert Burke, writing in *The Coming to Power: Critical Presidential Elections in American History,* Farley was disappointed to read frequent press reports that he was considered "ineligible for the presidency" by many people because of his religion.

When John F. Kennedy, a Catholic, entered the race for the 1960 Democratic nomination, party leaders were fearful, remembering what had happened to Al Smith. In what appeared to some to be a replay of the 1928 election, Kennedy was attacked by conservative Protestant ministers, and millions of pieces of hate mail against him were distributed.

But Kennedy was at least able to neutralize his Catholicism as a campaign issue by stressing the theme of fair play. Said Kennedy: "If I should lose on the real issues, I shall return to my seat in the Senate, satisfied that I tried my best and was fairly judged." Then he added, "But if this election is decided on the basis that forty million Americans lost their chance of being President on the day they were baptized, then it is the whole nation that will be the loser in the eyes of history, and in the eyes of our own people." Kennedy made it seem unfair for him to be judged on the basis of religion. It was a dramatic and powerful appeal. Kennedy captured the nomination and went on to defeat Richard Nixon in the election.

Kennedy boasted another quality that many candidates have demonstrated—persistence. He had the ability to shake off defeat and try again. Kennedy had made an attempt to win the vice-presidential nomination in 1956 and, while he did well in the voting, lost out to Estes Kefauver. Four years later Kennedy bounced back to capture the presidential nomination and the 1960 election.

There are many other examples of persistence paying off. The Republican candidate Richard M. Nixon lost to Kennedy in the 1960 presidential election. Nixon was also beaten in a bid for the governorship of California in 1962. However, Nixon's second attempt to

*John F. Kennedy had several hurdles to overcome before winning the
Democratic presidential nomination in 1960. Here, Kennedy holds a
press conference during the West Virginia primary.*

win the White House in the election of 1968 was successful.

Ronald Reagan, who became President in 1981, lost the Republican nomination in 1976 to Gerald R. Ford. And take what happened to George Bush. In 1964 and 1970, Bush lost in races for the United States Senate. Bush's first attempt to get nominated in 1980 was unsuccessful, when Reagan won. Bush persisted and won the 1988 election.

"This tells us two things," says Richard M. Pious, author of *The American Presidency*. "We like to humble our politicians before we elevate them. And our losers in one election can become winners in another."

Attitudes change. Once, being Catholic was a barrier to getting nominated and elected. Race was — and is — a problem today. But it is not as great a problem as it once was.

As of 1989, according to the Joint Center for Political Studies, there were 23 blacks serving in the United States House of Representatives (but none in the Senate), 301 black mayors, 1 black governor, 2,621 members of municipal governing boards, and 406 state legislators.

As for women, they now serve at every level of political office. As of 1989, there were 2 women senators and 25 serving in the House of Representatives. Approximately 1,200 women were serving in state legislatures. Said Irene Natividad, National Chair of the National Women's Political Caucus, "Voters are increasingly judging them [women] by their credentials rather than by their gender; a marked sign of progress."

The primary elections of 1988 also showed signs of progress. For instance, in the Wisconsin primary, won by Michael Dukakis, Jesse Jackson captured nearly 25 percent of the white vote, the most he won in any major primary. Said the *New York Times:* "For a time, and for the first time in American history, white voters of all beliefs and conditions seriously thought of voting for a black man for President of the United States."

Michael J. Robinson, associate professor of government at Georgetown University, called 1988 a "commendable" presidential election year. Said Robinson: "In the first six months, a black man ran for the presidency and none of his opponents made that an issue. We then nominated a Greek as a Democratic candidate [Michael Dukakis], and the Republicans did not make that an issue."

In the next presidential election, the Democratic and Republican candidates are almost certainly going to be male and white. But in elections to come, race and sex are not likely to be as important as they have been. The day when America's voters will support a woman or a black, Hispanic, or Asian for President may not be far off.

CHAPTER TEN

THE RUNNING MATE

Long before the nominating convention opens, every likely candidate has in mind the names of individuals who would make suitable running mates. Usually the nominee discusses these names with party leaders before a choice is made.

The Vice-President's legal qualifications are exactly the same as those of the President. The vice-presidential candidate must be at least 35 years old, a resident of the United States for fourteen years, and a natural-born citizen.

In practice, however, there are many other considerations. The Vice-President is often cho-sen because the person represents a state that is very important to the election. It is likely to be a state with a large electoral vote in which the outcome is regarded as being quite close. The vice-presidential candidate, by appealing to local loyalties, is expected to boost the party's chances in the state.

That was thought to be Michael Dukakis's thinking in 1988 when he selected Senator Lloyd Bentsen of Texas to be his running mate. Texas was crucial to the Democrats. Ever since Texas became a state in 1845, no Democrat had ever been elected President without carrying the state.

But the strategy backfired. Bentsen was also on the Texas ballot as a Senator running for reelection. So his Texan supporters were able to vote for him as a senatorial candidate, and at the same time also vote for Dukakis's Republican rival, George Bush, who claimed Texas as his home state.

Dukakis lost Texas by half a million votes and also lost the election. But his Texan supporters returned Bentsen to the Senate by a million-vote margin.

On other occasions, the vice-presidential candidate has been chosen because the person is believed to appeal to a large bloc of voters. In 1984, for example, when the Democrats made Walter F. Mondale their presidential nominee, they picked Representative Geraldine Ferraro of New York for Vice-President. She was the first woman ever chosen as the vice-presidential candidate by a major party. Despite her presence on the ticket, Republican candidates— Ronald Reagan and George Bush—carried a majority of the women who voted.

The vice-presidential choice is frequently made to "balance the ticket" and thus provide broader voter appeal. If, for example, the presidential candidate is a liberal, he or she may suggest a Vice-President who has some conservative leanings. A presidential nominee from a northeastern or midwestern state may pick a Vice-President from the South.

Ticket-balancing is not something new. After Abraham Lincoln was re-nominated by the Republicans in 1864, he turned to Andrew Johnson, a "war Democrat," to add strength to the ticket.

When sixty-two-year-old George Bush made his vice-presidential selection in 1988, he sought to balance the ticket with a much younger man. His choice was forty-one-year-old Senator Dan Quayle of Indiana.

In the week before the nominating convention, Bush had asked six or seven of his top advisers to list their three favorites for Vice-President. Quayle received more votes than anyone else. Bush

The Main Event
MONDALE/FERRARO
TOGETHER

NOV. 1 — 12 Noon
7 AV. & 37 ST.

BE THERE!
Volunteers call (212) 682-9680

Representative Geraldine Ferraro of New York, who ran with Walter F. Mondale in 1984, was the first woman ever chosen by a major party as a vice-presidential candidate.

George Bush (left) surprised many political observers and his own party when he named Dan Quayle as his running mate in 1988.

then asked for a background check on Senator Quayle, which showed nothing really harmful.

Bush's choice startled most observers. And in the days that followed the announcement, doubts about the young senator's qualifications were often heard. Democrats seized on Quayle's candidacy as a weak point in the Bush campaign. The controversy surrounding Quayle's selection got so hot that for a brief period Bush and his advisers considered dropping the young senator from the ticket and replacing him with someone else. That actually happened in 1972 when George McGovern, who had just been nominated by the Democrats, made Senator Thomas Eagleton of Missouri his vice-presidential selection. It seemed like a first-rate choice. Eagleton had strong backing from organized labor. He also came from a state that was going to be important to McGovern in the election. But shortly after the convention delegates confirmed Eagleton, it was revealed that he had experienced severe mental depression several times in the past and had been hospitalized for electric-shock treatments.

Although McGovern declared he wanted to keep the Missouri senator on the ticket and said he backed him "1000 percent," he eventually decided to ask Eagleton to resign. R. Sargent Shriver, who had once been director of the Peace Corps and ambassador to France, was chosen to take Eagleton's place.

McGovern was soundly defeated by Richard Nixon in the fall election. There were many reasons for McGovern's failure, but no one doubted the Eagleton affair hurt him badly.

The Republicans have had vice-presidential troubles of their own. They date to 1968 when the Republican presidential nominee made a startling choice for his running mate. Nixon had seen the results of polls that indicated all of the vice-presidential candidates would hurt his election chances more than they would help. So Nixon picked Spiro Agnew, the governor of Maryland, who was scarcely known outside of his own state. Immediately, the headlines asked: SPIRO AGNEW — WHO'S HE?

The Nixon-Agnew team was elected in 1968 and returned to office in 1972. But Agnew turned out to be a sorry choice.

In 1973, federal officials began to investigate charges that Agnew had accepted bribes from construction firms in return for helping them get government work in Maryland. The investigation covered an earlier period, when Agnew had been the Baltimore county executive and then governor of Maryland.

Although Agnew denied any wrongdoing, he resigned as Vice-President on October 10, 1973, under the terms of an agreement with the Department of Justice. He was permitted to plead nolo contendere (no contest) to a single charge — that he had cheated the federal government of $13,551 on his 1967 federal income tax payment. The judge stated the plea was "the full equivalent of a plea of guilty." Agnew was fined $10,000 and sentenced to three years probation.

It is often pointed out that the Vice-President is the position from which Presidents have been most frequently drawn. Eight Vice-Presidents have taken office upon the death of a President. Five were later elected to the Presidency. Gerald Ford succeeded to the presidency after Richard Nixon's resignation. That's fourteen Vice-

Presidents who have become President, or slightly more than one-third.

That statistic points up the importance of the office of the Vice-President. Because the person who occupies that office may one day be President, it is often said that much more care should go into the selection of vice-presidential candidates. The choice should not be left solely to the person who has just been nominated for the presidency and his advisers.

Those who wish to reform the system call for a screening committee to check the backgrounds and qualifications of all the men and women being considered for the office of Vice-President. Only the candidates who pass the investigation would be eligible for the office.

No matter how or for what reasons the vice-presidential candidate is chosen, he or she must be confirmed by the convention. The same balloting procedure is used as for the presidential candidate.

On the last night of the convention, the presidential nominee delivers a speech that is meant to inspire party workers and the vast television audience as well. Then the candidate brings out the vice-presidential nominee. The candidates' spouses join them on the podium. Party leaders also appear. They all raise their hands in triumph and the spectators cheer and applaud. But the moment is more a beginning than an end, for the election campaign lies just ahead.

CHAPTER ELEVEN

ROOM FOR IMPROVEMENT

For years, political experts criticized conventions for not reflecting the will of the voter. Too much power was concentrated in the hands of the party leaders. Deals were made behind the scenes that took away votes from one candidate and handed them to another.

The increased emphasis on primary elections has stilled this criticism. In a great majority of states, convention delegates now follow the wishes of the primary voters.

Another often-heard criticism was that conventions were undemocratic. They did not speak for women, for the poor, for blacks, or for minority ethnic groups. This problem has been confronted in recent years. As explained in Chapter Four, the Democratic party has, in fact, required each state party to submit a plan of "affirmative action"—action to be taken to provide equal opportunity for women and ethnic minorities in selecting convention delegates.

In 1980, the Democrats went a step further and set a requirement that one-half of the delegates at the national convention that year be women. If a faction had reason to believe that its state party was not abiding by the affirmative-action plan, the group could file a complaint with the party's Compliance Review Commission.

The new rules triggered enormous changes in the makeup of the Democratic party's leadership. In 1964, when the party held its convention in Atlantic City, black would-be delegates could not even get into the convention hall. In 1988, the Democratic party in Mississippi had a black chairman in Ed Cole. "Only 38 percent of the delegates in Atlanta [in 1988] are white men," noted the *New York Times*.

In more recent years, conventions have been criticized not for their lack of ethnic composition but for their dullness. Thanks to primary voting, the results of the conventions are known in advance. Conventions lack suspense and have become "staged activities," according to their critics.

Conventions are said to bore the general public. During the 1988 Democratic National Convention, Roone Arledge, president of ABC News, suggested that the Democrats and Republicans, perhaps in meetings with network officials, "come up with something more appealing." Said Arledge: "The political parties are turning off the American public."

This state of affairs caused a group of Democratic and Republican leaders to form a commission to examine conventions. Called the Commission on National Political Conventions, it planned to make recommendations to the two parties on how conventions can be made more interesting.

Frank J. Fahrenkopf, a one-time national chairman of the Republican Party, was named a co-chairman of the Commission. "One of the things we're going to be looking at," Fahrenkopf told the *Washington Post*, "is whether or not the convention process cannot be streamlined in some way, to make it crisper, make it cleaner from the standpoint of presenting a program that will attract more Americans to watch it."

Reformers are also looking for ways to improve the system of primaries and caucuses. It is frequently pointed out that candidates

Conventions of the future may be shorter and move faster than their predecessors but certain traditions, such as balloon showers, are not going to change. This is the scene at the Republican convention in 1956. Its nominee, Dwight D. Eisenhower (center), enjoys the spectacle.

often exhaust themselves by competing in thirty to forty primaries and caucuses over a period of six to seven months. Their budgets are also exhausted since many millions of dollars are required to run a campaign.

One solution offered is to create a national primary. All of those seeking to be nominated would compete on a single day of voting. Although the turnout for such an election would likely be lower than that for the November election, it would probably be greater than it is for the present combination of primaries and caucuses. It would also be much easier on the candidates and would not be nearly as costly.

But a national primary presents some problems. Unless free television were made available, a national primary would surely favor the best-known and best-financed candidates. Underdogs would have little chance of success.

One benefit of the present system is that it is a true screening process. Once the long and grueling primary season has ended, voters have a good idea of the strengths and weaknesses of the leading participants. The inept and poorly organized don't make it to the finish line.

A compromise between the present system and a national primary is implied by Super Tuesday, the day when many Southern states hold primaries. In election year 1988, Super Tuesday was a twenty-state event.

Super Tuesday suggests regional primaries. A series of such primaries might be held in each section of the United States: one in the South, one in New England, a third in the Midwest, a fourth on the West Coast, and so on. Several regional contests over two or three months would be less wearing on the candidates and less costly. They would be likely to attract as much voter interest as the present primaries do. And they would cause the candidates to undergo much the same critical analysis.

Caucuses are more heatedly criticized than primaries. In most, the turnout is low, lower than the primaries. Often, one group of activists competes against another group, with no widespread voter involvement.

Caucuses have been described as "easy prey for candidates with support from enthusiasts." Reformers have suggested fewer caucuses and have even recommended replacing the existing ones with primaries.

In the two centuries or so that Americans have been nominating and electing Presidents, the process has undergone significant change. Presidential nominations were once in the hands of congressional caucuses. Their power then passed to national party nominating conventions. When voters became dissatisfied with "boss rule," primary voting was instituted in many states. When women and minority groups protested they were poorly represented at national conventions, party leaders provided for a fairer mix of delegates.

In the past, the nation's political system has often responded to the people's call for change. It will again, if the voters of the future demand it.

PRESIDENTIAL ELECTIONS

Year	President Elected	Losing Candidate
1789	George Washington *(Federalist)*	(no opposition)
1792	George Washington *(Federalist)*	(no opposition)
1796	John Adams *(Federalist)*	Thomas Jefferson *(Democrat-Republican)*
1800	Thomas Jefferson *(Democrat-Republican)*	Aaron Burr *(Democrat-Republican)*
1804	Thomas Jefferson *(Democrat-Republican)*	Charles Pinckney *(Federalist)*
1808	James Madison *(Democrat-Republican)*	Charles Pinckney *(Federalist)*

1812	James Madison *(Democrat-Republican)*	DeWitt Clinton *(Federalist)*
1816	James Monroe *(Democrat-Republican)*	Rufus King *(Federalist)*
1820	James Monroe *(Democrat-Republican)*	John Quincy Adams *(Democrat-Republican)*
1824	John Quincy Adams *(Democrat-Republican)*	Andrew Jackson *(Democrat-Republican)* Henry Clay *(Democrat-Republican)* William H. Crawford *(Democrat-Republican)*
1828	Andrew Jackson *(Democrat)*	John Quincy Adams *(National Republican)*
1832	Andrew Jackson *(Democrat)*	Henry Clay *(National Republican)*
1836	Martin Van Buren *(Democrat)*	William H. Harrison *(Whig)*
1840	William H. Harrison *(Whig)*	Martin Van Buren *(Democrat)*
1844	James K. Polk *(Democrat)*	Henry Clay *(Whig)*
1848	Zachary Taylor *(Whig)*	Lewis Cass *(Democrat)*
1852	Franklin Pierce *(Democrat)*	Winfield Scott *(Whig)*

1856	James C. Buchanan *(Democrat)*	John C. Frémont *(Republican)*
1860	Abraham Lincoln *(Republican)*	Stephen A. Douglas *(Democrat)* John C. Breckinridge *(Democrat)* John Bell *(Constitutional Union)*
1864	Abraham Lincoln *(Republican)*	George McClellan *(Democrat)*
1868	Ulysses S. Grant *(Republican)*	Horatio Seymour *(Democrat)*
1872	Ulysses S. Grant *(Republican)*	Horace Greeley *(Democrat-Liberal Republican)*
1876	Rutherford B. Hayes *(Republican)*	Samuel J. Tilden *(Democrat)*
1880	James A. Garfield *(Republican)*	Winfield S. Hancock *(Democrat)*
1884	Grover Cleveland *(Democrat)*	James G. Blaine *(Republican)*
1888	Benjamin Harrison *(Republican)*	Grover Cleveland *(Democrat)*
1892	Grover Cleveland *(Democrat)*	Benjamin Harrison *(Republican)* James Weaver *(People's Party)*

1896	William McKinley *(Republican)*	William J. Bryan *(Democrat, People's Party)*
1900	William McKinley *(Republican)*	William J. Bryan *(Democrat)*
1904	Theodore Roosevelt *(Republican)*	Alton B. Parker *(Democrat)*
1908	William H. Taft *(Republican)*	William J. Bryan *(Democrat)*
1912	Woodrow Wilson *(Democrat)*	Theodore Roosevelt *(Progressive)* William H. Taft *(Republican)*
1916	Woodrow Wilson *(Democrat)*	Charles E. Hughes *(Republican)*
1920	Warren G. Harding *(Republican)*	James M. Cox *(Democrat)*
1924	Calvin Coolidge *(Republican)*	John W. Davis *(Democrat)* Robert M. LaFollette *(Progressive)*
1928	Herbert Hoover *(Republican)*	Alfred E. Smith *(Democrat)*
1932	Franklin D. Roosevelt *(Democrat)*	Herbert Hoover *(Republican)* Norman Thomas *(Socialist)*

1936	Franklin D. Roosevelt *(Democrat)*	Alfred Landon *(Republican)*
1940	Franklin D. Roosevelt *(Democrat)*	Wendell Willkie *(Republican)*
1944	Franklin D. Roosevelt *(Democrat)*	Thomas E. Dewey *(Republican)*
1948	Harry S. Truman *(Democrat)*	Thomas E. Dewey *(Republican)* J. Strom Thurmond *(State's Rights)* Henry A. Wallace *(Progressive)*
1952	Dwight D. Eisenhower *(Republican)*	Adlai E. Stevenson *(Democrat)*
1956	Dwight D. Eisenhower *(Republican)*	Adlai E. Stevenson *(Democrat)*
1960	John F. Kennedy *(Democrat)*	Richard M. Nixon *(Republican)*
1964	Lyndon B. Johnson *(Democrat)*	Barry M. Goldwater *(Republican)*
1968	Richard M. Nixon *(Republican)*	Hubert H. Humphrey *(Democrat)* George Wallace *(Progressive)*
1972	Richard M. Nixon *(Republican)*	George McGovern *(Democrat)*

1976	Jimmy Carter *(Democrat)*	Gerald R. Ford *(Republican)*
1980	Ronald Reagan *(Republican)*	Jimmy Carter *(Democrat)* John B. Anderson *(Independent)*
1984	Ronald Reagan *(Republican)*	Walter F. Mondale *(Democrat)*
1988	George Bush *(Republican)*	Michael S. Dukakis *(Democrat)*

GLOSSARY

affirmative action   Action taken to provide equal opportunity for minority groups and women, as in the makeup of state convention delegations.

balance the ticket   A party's way of combining presidential and vice-presidential candidates so that broader voter appeal is provided and varied interests are represented.

ballot   A device such as a sheet of paper by which a voter registers a choice in an election.

bandwagon   A political campaign that attracts an ever increasing number of supporters.

boss   A leader with great power within a political party; bosses often manipulate voting and elections.

candidate   An individual who seeks or is nominated for political office.

caucus   A meeting of small groups of party members for the purpose of deciding questions of policy or selecting a candidate for elective office.

closed primary A primary election in which only registered members of that political party can vote for candidates on their party's ballot. The primary is closed to all others.

conservative A political point of view. Conservatives are generally traditionalists. They have a narrow view of what government can achieve. Conservatives are generally opposed to high taxes and big spending programs.

convention A formal meeting of members of a party to nominate candidates to run for President or other political offices.

dark horse A little-known candidate who receives unexpected support at a nominating convention.

delegate A representative to a convention.

delegation A group of persons representing a district or state.

draft To nominate a candidate because of pressure exerted by party members or large numbers of voters.

election Organized voting to choose a candidate for office.

elector The individuals chosen by the voters to elect the President and Vice-President. Each state has a certain number of electors; the number is the same as the total of the state's senators and representatives.

electoral college The body of presidential electors chosen in each state and the District of Columbia every four years to elect the President and Vice-President of the United States. To win a presidential election, a candidate must claim a majority of the electoral votes.

electoral vote The vote cast by members of the electoral college.

electorate   A body of qualified voters.

favorite son   A person backed as a presidential candidate by his or her own state delegates at a national political convention.

flier   A political pamphlet or circular for mass distribution. Fliers are an important part of any political campaign and are usually handed out by volunteers.

Framers of the Constitution   The individuals who helped formulate the ideas contained in the Constitution at the time of its writing in 1787. Included in the group were Alexander Hamilton, James Madison, John Jay, and Benjamin Franklin.

general election   An election involving most or all of the nation's political parties and their foremost candidates.

inauguration   The formal ceremony, including the taking of the oath, that takes place at the beginning of a President's term of office.

incumbent   A person holding a particular political office.

independent voter   A voter who does not belong to a political party.

landslide   An overwhelming political victory.

legislature   A body of persons with the power to make laws for a state, nation, or other political unit.

liberals   A political point of view. Liberals generally look to the federal government to play an active role in solving social problems. Liberals usually support such social welfare programs as unemployment insurance and antipoverty legislation.

local election   An election involving city, county, or town offices.

major party   The Democratic or Republican party.

majority   A number that is more than half of the total number.

matching funds   Money for a political campaign provided by the federal government or other source that is equal in amount to funds that come through private donations.

media   Television, radio, newspapers, magazines, and other means of mass communication; an important tool in present-day politics and political campaigns.

minor party   *See* **third party.**

National Committee   A group of people chosen by a political party that selects the national chairperson and helps him or her run the party, including the making of plans for the next national convention. In the case of the Democratic and Republican parties, the national committee consists of a man and woman from each state and territory, plus the District of Columbia.

national convention   The convention held every four years by a major party to nominate candidates for President and Vice-President; the symbol of politics in the United States.

nominate   To propose as a candidate.

open primary   A primary election open to all voters, not merely those registered with a particular party.

party   A political group organized to support its principles and candidates for public office and ultimately to gain control of the running of the government.

plank   One section of a political party's platform devoted to a specific issue.

platform   A statement of a party's stands on major issues of the day; the party platform is unveiled during the party's national convention.

politics   The art and science of gaining elective office; also, the activities and affairs of a political party.

poll   *See* **public opinion poll.**

polls   The place where votes are cast in an election.

pollster   A person who takes a public opinion poll.

popular vote   The votes cast by the voters at large.

precinct   An election district in a city or town; the smallest local unit within the organization of a political party.

primary election   A preliminary election in which members of a party in a state vote to select delegates to the party's national convention. The delegates in turn cast their ballots for the voters' choice. Depending on the state, the primary election may also involve party members in a state choosing a candidate.

public opinion poll   A survey of a sample of the public to obtain information or record opinion.

registered voter   A person who is eligible to vote by means of formally enrolling his or her name with a precinct.

representative   A member of the House of Representatives, the lower house of the United States Congress. Representatives are usually called congressmen or congresswomen. The number of representatives elected by each state is proportionate to the state's population.

roll call The reading aloud of a list of delegations at a national convention so that each may vote and have its vote registered.

senator A member of the Senate, the upper house of the United States Congress. Two senators are elected from each state.

super delegate A delegate to a national convention who is appointed by the party, not elected. Super delegates have included senators, representatives, and high party officials.

Super Tuesday The second Tuesday in March of a presidential election year when a large group of Southern states hold their primaries. Super Tuesday was planned to give Southern voters more of a say in the nomination process.

third party A party organized as an alternative to the two major parties; also called a minor party.

ticket The list of candidates offered by a party in an election; also called a slate.

unit rule A voting rule permitted by the Democratic party at its presidential nominating convention from 1860 to 1968. Under unit rule, the entire vote of a state delegation had to be cast for the candidate preferred by the majority, even though a portion of the delegation members might favor another candidate.

volunteer A person who works for a party or a party's candidate without being paid; often, volunteers are the closest link between a party and the voters.

write-in vote A vote cast by writing in the name of a candidate not on the ballot.

FURTHER READING

Boller, Paul F., Jr. *Presidential Campaigns*. New York: Oxford University Press, 1984.

Clemente, Frank and Frank Watkins, eds. *Keep Hope Alive: Jesse Jackson's 1988 Presidential Campaign*. Boston: South End Press, 1989.

Crouse, Timothy. *The Boys on the Bus: Riding with the Campaign Press Corps*. New York: Ballantine, 1986.

Drew, Elizabeth. *Election Journal: The Political Events of 1987–1988*. New York: Morrow, 1989.

Ferguson, Thomas, ed. *The Hidden Election: Politics and Economics in the 1980 Presidential Campaign*. New York: Pantheon, 1982.

Geer, John G. *Nominating Presidents: An Evaluation of Voters and Primaries*. Westport, Conn.: Greenwood Press, 1989.

Germond, Jack W. and Jules Witcover. *Whose Broad Stripes and Bright Stars? The Trivial Pursuit of the Presidency, 1988.* New York: Warner Brooks, 1989.

Goldman, Peter and Tom Matthews. *The Quest for the Presidency, 1988.* New York: Simon & Schuster, 1989.

Hiebert, Ray E., et al., eds. *The Political Image Merchants: Strategies for the Seventies.* Reston, Va.: Acropolis Books, 1975.

Kronenwetter, Michael. *Politics and the Press.* New York: Franklin Watts, 1987.

League of Women Voters of the United States. Education Fund. *Choosing the President.* Nashville: Thomas Nelson, 1980.

Matthews, Christopher. *Hardball: How Politics is Played — Told by One Who Knows the Game.* New York: Harper & Row, 1989.

McGinniss, Joe. *Selling of the President, 1968.* New York: Pocket Books, 1984.

Polsby, Nelson W. and Aaron Wildavsky. *Presidential Elections: Contemporary Strategies of American Electoral Politics.* New York: The Free Press, 1988.

Reiter, Howard L. *Selecting the President: The Nominating Process in Transition.* Philadelphia: University of Pennsylvania Press, 1985.

Samuels, Cynthia K. *It's a Free Country! A Young Person's Guide to Politics and Elections.* New York: Atheneum, 1988.

Schlesinger, Arthur M., Jr. and Fred L. Israel, eds. *The Coming to Power: Critical Presidential Elections in American History.* New York: Chelsea House, 1981.

Schlesinger, Arthur M., Jr. *History of American Presidential Elections, 1972–1984.* New York: Chelsea House, 1986.

Shafer, Byron E. *Quiet Revolution: The Struggle for the Democratic Party and the Shaping of Post-Reform Politics.* New York: Russell Sage Foundation, 1983.

Sheehy, Gail. *Character: America's Search for Leadership.* New York: Morrow, 1988.

Simon, Paul. *Winners and Losers, The 1988 Race for the Presidency — One Candidate's Perspective.* New York: Continuum, 1989.

Simon, Roger. *Road Show: In America, Anyone Can Become President. It's One of the Risks We Take.* New York: Farrar, Straus and Giroux, 1990.

Taylor, Paul. *See How They Run: Electing the President in an Age of Mediaocracy.* New York: Knopf, 1990.

Wattenberg, Martin P. *The Rise of Candidate-Centered Politics: Presidential Elections in the 1980s.* Cambridge, Mass.: Harvard University Press, 1991.

Wayne, Stephen J. *The Road to the White House: The Politics of Presidential Elections.* New York: St. Martin's Press, 1987.

White, Theodore H. *America in Search of Itself: The Making of the President 1956–1980.* New York: Harper & Row, 1982.

Will, George F. *The New Season: A Spectator's Guide to the 1988 Election.* New York: Simon & Schuster, 1988.

Witcover, Jules. *Eighty-Five Days: The Last Campaign of Robert Kennedy.* New York: Morrow, 1988.

Witcover, Jules. *Marathon: The Pursuit of the Presidency 1972–1976.* New York: Viking Press, 1977.

ACKNOWLEDGMENTS

Special thanks are due Richard M. Pious, Professor of Political Science at Barnard College, Columbia University, New York, New York, for his careful reading of the manuscript and his thoughtful suggestions. He played a valuable role.

The author is also grateful to Kevin Coleman, Congressional Research Service, the Library of Congress; Ludwiga Barabas, the Robert A. Taft Institute of Government; Lillie Murdock, the Republican National Committee; Rick Boylan, the Democratic National Committee; Kelly Mills, Turner Broadcasting System; Donna Yorke, ABC Television; Judy Kittleson, the Churches' Committee for Voter Registration; Patricia M. Frierson, Vote America; Yasmin Cader, National Coalition on Black Voter Participation; David Stanhope, Jimmy Carter Library; Richard L. Holzhausen, Gerald R. Ford Library; Martin M. Teasley, Dwight D. Eisenhower Library; E. Philip Scott, Lyndon Baines Johnson Library; Susan Y. Elter, Franklin D. Roosevelt Library; Allan B. Goodrich, John Fitzgerald Kennedy Library; Benedict K. Zobrist, Harry S. Truman Library; Francesca Kurti, TLC Labs; Ann Hagen Griffiths, Brian Kathenes, and Tim Sullivan.

PHOTO ACKNOWLEDGMENTS

AP/Wide World: 71, 73, 78. Board of Elections, City of New York: 57. Capital Cities/ABC, Inc.: 85. Jimmy Carter Library: 75. Democratic National Committee: 89. Dwight D. Eisenhower Library: 91, 102, 118. Harper's Weekly: 31. Internal Revenue Service: 65. Lyndon B. Johnson Library: 43, 86. John F. Kennedy Library: 108. New Alliance Party/Omowale-Ketu Oladuwa: 51. New York Public Library: 15. Theodore Roosevelt Collection; Harvard College Library: 33. George Sullivan: 12, 21, 22, 27, 30, 35, 40, 41, 44, 48, 54, 64, 74, 80, 97, 98, 104, 105, 112. The White House/Michael Evans: 58, Pete Souza: 92, David Valdez: vi, 113.

INDEX

ABOUT
THE
AUTHOR

George Sullivan is a well-known author of books for children and young adults, with more than one hundred titles to his credit. Before becoming a full-time author in the mid-1960s, Mr. Sullivan worked in public relations and in publishing. Before that he served in the navy as a journalist. He grew up in Springfield, Massachusetts, and graduated from Fordham University in New York City.

His many interests are reflected in his writings. Subjects of his popular biographies for young readers have included Mikhail Gorbachev, Egyptian president Anwar Sadat, Ronald Reagan, and George Bush.